D1259147

The Naval Profession

BOOKS BY REAR ADMIRAL CALVERT

The Naval Profession

Surface at the Pole

FOR CHILDREN

A Promise to Our Country

The Naval Profession

REAR ADMIRAL JAMES CALVERT, U.S.N.

McGraw-Hill Book Company
New York Toronto London

Printed in the United States of America.

Library of Congress Catalog Card Number: 65-24890
FIRST EDITION
09656

The opinions or assertions contained herein are the private
ones of the writer and are not to be construed as official, or as reflecting
the views of the Navy Department or the naval service at large.

To Nancy

Acknowledgment

The professional outlook and viewpoint of a naval officer are shaped to a considerable extent by those officers and men with whom he has served. At this writing I can remember at least a score who have significantly influenced my views. Some are older than I am, some younger; most know who they are with no word from me. To each of them, special thanks are due because it was largely they who molded the outlook I have attempted to set forth in this book.

I have made no pretense to original research, and the citing of specific reference material would be inappropriate. I have drawn liberally on those works listed in the bibliography at the back of this book as well as on other works concerning the Navy.

I would like to thank three fellow naval officers for their direct help. Rear Admiral William P. Mack, the Navy's Chief of Information, gave me valuable encouragement concerning the soundness of the approach I had taken to my subject. Captain Sheldon Kinney, Commandant of Midshipmen, read the section concerning the Naval Academy and made several corrections and additions. Finally, Captain Edward L. Beach, of the Office of the Chief of Naval Operations, read the entire manuscript and made many useful suggestions.

Any errors of fact which remain are solely my responsibility. It goes without saying that the views and opinions expressed are mine alone.

JAMES CALVERT

Preface

It was not long ago that a career as an officer in the armed forces was the choice of only a small number of men in this country each year. The route to a commission was mainly through West Point and Annapolis, and appointments were scarce.

Today an altogether different situation exists. Not only are there now three service academies, each accepting classes of increased size, but there are many other roads to a commission. The Navy alone commissions nearly 10,000 new officers each year to fill its needs, and maintains sixteen different programs aside from the Naval Academy for the procurement and training of these officers. One of these, the Naval Reserve Officers Training Corps, is established in more than fifty of the nation's colleges and universities, and produces some 2000 new officers for the Navy every year. The Officer Candidate School at Newport takes several thousand college graduates with no previous military experience and, after a sixteen-week indoctrination course, commissions them as ensigns in the Navy. The Navy's aviation programs, centered in Pensacola, Florida, produce over 1500 new officers for the service annually.

These large and varied programs provide so many opportunities for an education, for training, and for a commission that many of today's high school and college students contemplating them are overwhelmed and confused. I have often been asked to explain these programs, and something about the Navy, to groups of students. I have tried, but the compass of a short talk does not permit adequate coverage of this subject. I became convinced that a book was needed, describing those aspects of the Navy of interest to a young man about to enter one of its officer training programs.

It is not only among students contemplating the Navy from outside that questions arise. Midshipmen, officer candidates, aviation cadets, and even newly commissioned officers have questions about the life of a naval officer, about the naval profession, and about the Navy itself. Some of these young men know without any doubt that the Navy is the career they want; others are just as sure that their relationship with the Navy will be a temporary one. But many—perhaps the majority—are not so sure. They would like to know more about it before they make up their minds.

It is to all who would like to know more about the naval officer's profession—whether they contemplate the Navy from outside, are in training for a commission, or have already received one—that this book is addressed. I have attempted to set forth an objective description of the naval profession as it appears to an officer of longer—but by no means complete—experience.

Although it is somewhat unusual for a book about the Navy to be written by an officer still on active duty, I am convinced that it is almost necessary in this case. An officer still on active duty sees the naval officer's career from a point of view significantly different from that of the retired officer. He is, after all, still embroiled in the struggle. Doubts and tensions are still in the air. That sense of completeness and, perhaps, self-satisfaction accompanying retirement is not his. He must communicate, as it were, from midstream; and his impressions and views may be the most direct answer to a young man who wants to know what it's like to be a naval officer.

Both as a midshipman and as a young officer, I read many books about the Navy in an attempt to find out something about the naval profession, about what naval officers do on board various ships, how they are educated, how their families live, and what their traditions are. I never quite found the book I wanted.

I hope this book will fill that void for others.

JC

Norfolk
May, 1965

Contents

CHAPTER ONE

What Is the Navy?

During my plebe year at Annapolis, more years ago than I like to remember accurately, an old four-stacked destroyer visited the Naval Academy for a weekend. It was the first ship of the Navy I had ever seen except in photographs, and I was anxious to go on board for a visit.

The four-pipers were not the most glamorous ships the Navy has ever owned. Built hurriedly for World War I, they were of excellent design but austere, to put it gently. Many of them (and this one included) had spent most of the 1920s and 1930s laid up in the back channel, unmanned and neglected. In the late 1930s, with the threat of another war, they were being resurrected and once more commissioned as warships of the United States.

It was a hot, muggy day in August. The sun beat down on old Santee Wharf with that merciless strength it possesses on the Chesapeake on a windless, cloudless, summer day. Not a ripple disturbed the surface of the Severn River as it stretched with a metallic gleam toward the Bay. One listless knockabout drooped in mid-river with its sails limp on its old-fashioned gaff rig.

I walked up the deserted wooden wharf alone and noticed no activity on board the destroyer to disturb the sleepy afternoon. As I drew closer to the four-piper I could see that her wrinkled and battered hull plates had been hastily and poorly painted. I noted with some admiration, however, the way her huge white bow numbers had been expertly shaded with black to make them stand out against the gray of the hull.

I saluted the officer of the deck and asked permission to look around the ship. The young officer who had been left with the duty while his more fortunate shipmates went ashore did a poor job of concealing his amazement that anyone would want to so spend his time unless required. However, he recovered and told me to go right ahead if that was what I wanted.

Alone, I doggedly undertook to tour the ship from stem to stern. My firsthand knowledge of the Navy was nil. Still, the equipment of the old ship was so simple that I had little trouble identifying most of the things I saw. I stopped awhile to talk with a young sailor who sat dejectedly peeling potatoes for the evening meal. He was not much for talk, however, and I received little information beyond the fact that the ship had only recently been placed back in commission and "wasn't straightened out yet."

Agreeing with this irrefutable observation, I continued my tour. Finally, I arrived on the bridge. Here things were more shipshape, and brightwork polish had even been applied in some of the more conspicuous places. The decrepit quality of the rest of the ship was temporarily dispelled.

A lieutenant in a rather tired-looking white uniform was leaning over the chart table, studying some sort of loose-leaf book.

"Down to look her over, eh?" he asked in a friendly tone. "Well, what do you think?"

"Well . . . ," I began.

The lieutenant fixed me with a serious look. He cleared his throat as though he were about to make an important pronouncement. "I'm glad," he said, "that you are down here to see the ship." He paused a bit for emphasis and then went on. "Because *this is the Navy*."

I can still remember the words as though they had been spoken an hour ago, and the sinking sensation I felt in the pit of my stomach at hearing them. If this is really the Navy, I thought. . . .

The lieutenant, of course, was wrong. The old four-piper was not the Navy. It wasn't, as I know now, even a very good example of a Navy ship. And no ship, or combination of ships, can be called the Navy.

The Navy has been defined in many different ways. In the most general terms, it is the organization charged with exerting the power of the United States upon the seas of the world. Its mission is to control those seas so that we may use them as required in our national interest—and deny their use to others if necessary. More concretely, it is an organization of several hundred ships, several thousand airplanes, several hundred thousand men and women, and many shore establishments operating on an annual budget measured in billions of dollars.

It owns and operates training, educational, and research organizations. Its domestic influence is felt in every corner of the land, while its military influence reaches almost every part of the world. It supports research on subjects ranging from the language of porpoises to the radiation-absorption cross section of nuclear materials. It has officers who are specialists in subjects that reach from religion to criminal law, from economics to orthopedics, and from civil engineering to journalism. It holds positions for hundreds of thousands of civilian workers, running from sweepers and dusters up to highly trained metallurgical engineers and naval architects.

The lieutenant, I believe, was very wrong. There is no single place one can visit to see the Navy. There is no one person or book that can tell you all about the Navy. Its activities are so varied, its sweep so wide, that men of almost every sort, of almost every specialized interest, can find within it a place for themselves. At this very minute there are Navy men at sea under arduous and difficult circumstances, fighting the elements and darkness as seagoing men have done for centuries. But there are also studious-looking Navy men attending classes at M.I.T. or studying at the Navy's own graduate school in California. Every Sunday afternoon finds groups of young naval officers and their dates gathering around the clubs for tennis and golf—but those same Sunday afternoons see worried groups of captains and admirals gathering in the Pentagon for long, tedious meetings. There is no place on earth where one can put his hand and say, "This is the Navy."

Still, in all this vast complex of activities, there is one factor that touches the Navy in each of its facets and gives it a certain flavor which no advance of technology or change in social environment can ever erase—and that is the sea.

Man is a land animal, but his involvement with the sea reaches back into the very stuff and substance of his nature. In some dim Paleozoic age, long before mammals first appeared, the first life came hesitantly from the sea and attempted the great adventure of living on the land. Each creature since—amphibian, reptile, bird, or mammal—has carried in its veins a fluid which is closely linked to the actual components of sea water. Each of us has, in a very literal sense, the sea in his blood.

But the tie is more than chemical. Our civilization grew up around the Mediterranean Sea. It was at once the center of the world (as its name quite literally states) and the highway of its transportation. Across it the ancients sent their commerce and their ships of war. Across its "wine-dark" surface sped Homer's ships, and on it Paul's terrified shipmates cast out their stern anchors and prayed for daylight. Beyond the Gates of Hercules stretched another vast sea whose exploration would have to wait for a later age.

Throughout our conscious history the sea has offered a challenge of danger, adventure, and the possibility of profit. As our knowledge has increased our exploration of its limits and depths has become more bold. The sailing ship, the compass, the astrolabe, the chronometer, the sextant, the steam engine, the submarine, the aircraft carrier, and most recently, nuclear energy—each of these has marked an important change in the manner and efficiency with which man has been able to use the sea for commercial and national purposes. But through it all has run the bright thread of danger. The ancients drew their ships up on the beaches of the Mediterranean at night because they had learned to fear the night storm at sea. Columbus and his men chanted prayers as they changed the watches on their tiny caravels and sailed uncertainly to the west. And the tragedy of the *Thresher* has reminded us that, with all our modern knowledge and wondrous mechanisms, the ancient and elemental power of the sea remains unchanged.

The constant exposure to the sea with its challenge, its dangers, and its rewards has given the Navy a tradition that is distinctly its own. It is a tradition of self-reliance and self-discipline—of self-confidence if you will. It is a tradition of respect for the power of the elements and of the importance of a single life in danger on the sea. It is a tradition that has not been without its effect on the character of America.

The history of the United States has been entwined with the sea from the beginning. The discovery of our land began with great sea adventures. In our mind's eye we can still see red-bearded Leif Ericson at the helm of his open Viking ship with its graceful prow, peering through the mist and spray at the dim coasts of the new world. Five centuries later and many miles to the south, Christopher Columbus and his men touched at an inconsequential tropical isle and thereby opened the great continents of the Western Hemisphere to European civilization.

For centuries after Columbus, the Atlantic bore the warp and woof of American culture and tradition across from the mother lands of Europe. Seaborne commerce was vital to the early growth of our country; in the middle of the nineteenth century the whaling industry brought American commercial enterprise and seafaring skill together in one of their most colorful blends. Living for two and three years at a stretch in shipboard conditions we can now only faintly imagine, the Yankee whalers explored the reaches of the South Seas, probed the Arctic Ocean, and brought back to their crisp white houses in Nantucket and New Bedford both riches and a renewed sense of that self-reliance which is the hallmark of men who are at home upon the sea.

As exploration and commerce have given our nation its birth and its sinews, so the use of the sea has helped to preserve them through the perils of war. Sea power was important in the defeat of Cornwallis at Yorktown, and what few bright chapters existed for us in the War of 1812 were written on the seas. Although overshadowed by bloody battles on the land, there were stirring sea tales for both sides to relate at the end of the Civil War.

The marriage of American industrial power and the Navy was preceded by a long and fitfully unhappy engagement; we were slow in developing the steel-and-steam warship in our Navy. When the supreme test finally came, however, in the sea war with Japan, it found the Navy ready and equipped with ships that incorporated all the strength and skill of American industrial and scientific enterprise. It is well that it did, for in that war of the 1940s the Navy needed all the power that American industry and science could give it. In that war, the Navy fired more shots, sank more ships, lost more ships, had more men killed, and conducted more operations than in all its previous history combined.

Important as ships are, however, naval history is made by men. John Paul Jones winning his desperate slugging match with the *Serapis* . . . the dashing young Stephen Decatur gliding into Tripoli harbor under cover of night to burn the captured *Philadelphia* . . . David Farragut expressing his scorn for the Confederate mines at Mobile Bay . . . the brave young aviators avenging Pearl Harbor by sinking all four of the Japanese carriers at the Battle of Midway—these are only a few of the bright moments in the history of the American naval profession. And behind these and the other Navy men whom history has immortalized have been thousands of unknowns, just as professional, just as devoted to the aims to which this great organization is dedicated.

It is my hope in this book to evoke something of the spirit and ideals of the American naval profession, to attempt to identify those characteristics which distinguish it from other careers, and perhaps to shed some light on what the future might hold for young men contemplating its pursuit today. I write fully realizing the importance of teamwork among all our military services—indeed, among all agencies of our government—in the modern world. Nevertheless, our nation has, after careful consideration, concluded that separate military services, trained to work together, should be maintained—each service keeping its traditions and its own expertise as ingredients of the national defense system.

If our system is to work to best advantage, each military service must have its devoted professionals who, while understanding and respecting the role of the other services, remain experts in their own field. A young man contemplating a career in the uniform of his nation must think in terms of a specific service; he wants to be a naval officer, a Marine, or an Air Force or Army officer. This book is, without further apology, addressed to those whose interest, for whatever reason, is the Navy.

The Department of the Navy includes two military services: the Navy and the Marine Corps. No naval officer can serve as long as I have without developing a deep and lasting admiration for the Marines. However, I have omitted them from this book for a very sound reason: I am attempting to describe a profession from within so that those who contemplate its pursuit may have some help and guidance. I cannot do this for the Marines; I have not lived their life and I cannot, with any degree of authority, describe their profession. I must leave that task to one of their own.

There is one other omission which must be explained. In the chapters which follow I have not undertaken to explain the nature and importance of the enlisted personnel of the Navy. There is nothing the Navy undertakes or accomplishes which could be done without these fine men and women. Their omission stems only from the necessity of focusing attention on one aspect of the Navy if I am to accomplish my aim.

CHAPTER TWO

What Does the Navy Do?

Our first order of business ought to be to describe what the Navy actually does. What is its purpose in peacetime? In war? How does it spend its money and time from day to day, from month to month? What, in short, is its job?

These questions about the Navy cannot be answered except in terms of the nation it serves. The Navy is an instrument of the United States; it exists to provide one of the means of attaining its national objectives. What are these objectives? Of the many possible answers, these few seem to me basic:

1. To maintain our way of life—particularly as it regards the dignity and freedom of the individual.
2. To maintain and, if possible, to improve our standard of living by taking intelligent steps to broaden the base and increase the vigor of our economy.
3. To maintain peace and create, insofar as possible, an atmosphere in which all nations may work together for the eventual achievement of a world in which individual nations need not maintain armed forces.

Freedom, prosperity, and peace. Few would argue with the desirability of such objectives. But how can the United States, only one nation among many, in a world community without world law, work effectively toward such lofty goals? The answer is, at best, a partial one. We, as a people, working through our government, must make wise decisions and create sound policies. We must blend a practical sense of self-preservation with as much idealism as is appropriate to the particular problem at hand.

Wise decisions and sound policies are not, however, enough by themselves. The United States must have strength to give substance to its policies; it must have force to protect itself and make its influence felt. Most reasonable men hope for a day when this will not be the case. But be that as it may, we are dealing with today's world. Objectives, policies, and goals—no matter how lofty from our point of view—are but empty words when they lack the means of attainment.

Armed force, of and by itself, is intrinsically neither good nor bad. Employed for constructive purposes in the pursuit of a creative foreign policy, it is fundamental to the achievement of our ultimate world goals, and thus is as valuable and important as the ideals for which we strive.

The part that the Navy plays within the United States Armed Forces cannot be explained without reference to the Department of Defense.

Although our nation possessed a Joint Board for Army and Navy cooperation as long ago as 1903, it took the massive campaigns of World War II to bring about the unified command structure of today. The National Security Act of 1947 formally established the Joint Chiefs of Staff and started a chain of legislation which eventually resulted in the structure of today, in which the Secretary of Defense acts directly under the President to control all the fighting forces of the United States.

There are seven unified commanders located throughout the world. Each is responsible for certain geographical areas; each commands essentially all of the fighting forces deployed within his area—regardless of the uniform he himself wears. The seven unified commands are:

U.S. European Command with headquarters in Paris
U.S. South Command with headquarters in the Canal Zone
U.S. Atlantic Command with headquarters in Norfolk
U.S. Pacific Command with headquarters in Hawaii
U.S. Alaskan Command with headquarters in Anchorage
U.S. Continental Air Defense Command with headquarters in Colorado Springs
U.S. Strike Command with headquarters in Florida

The Strike Command, charged with supplying troops and air power wherever the United States might need them, can also, under certain circumstances, have area responsibilities in the Middle East and parts of Africa.

Supplementing these seven commanders, there is the Strategic Air Command with headquarters in Omaha, which, although it consists only of Air Force units, reports directly to the Secretary of Defense as though it were a unified command. It is termed a *specified command.*

The entire structure of U.S. armed force hangs upon these eight commands and their subordinates. It is a remarkably flexible and effective system which makes our operating forces all over the world instantly responsive to the Secretary of Defense. The Secretary is authorized to, and does, delegate much of this command authority to the Joint Chiefs of Staff who, in turn, deal directly with the unified and specified commands. The fundamental command responsibility, however, rests with the Secretary of Defense.

This organization makes it possible for the President, acting through the Secretary of Defense, to bring joint (all services) action to bear anywhere in the world on very short notice and under close control. Although the top command is thoroughly unified, the individual military departments–Army, Navy, and Air Force–retain their identity farther down the chain of command. Theirs is the responsibility to equip, train, and organize the forces which will ultimately be given operational tasks by the unified and specified commanders. Each of the military departments is headed by its own civilian secretary and its own service chief (who doubles as that service's member of the Joint Chiefs of Staff); each has its own structure for discharging its responsibilities. The goal of all, however, is joint action under the unified command structure.

It should be apparent from the above discussion that teamwork among the services is not just a catch phrase; it is the main thrust of our defense effort throughout the world. But the purpose of this book is to discuss the naval officer's profession, and having very briefly set the Department of the Navy within its context in the Armed Forces, we will now focus our attention upon it.

The Department of the Navy consists of three parts:

1. The *Navy Department* (as distinguished from the Department of the Navy), which is, essentially, the Washington headquarters of the Navy. In this department are the Office of the Secretary, the Office of the Chief of Naval Operations, the headquarters of the Marine Corps, and the bureaus, boards, and offices which supply and administer the Navy.

2. The *operating forces* which consist, basically, of the ships and aircraft of the Navy and the crews who man them.

3. The *shore establishment*, which consists of the bases, supply depots, repair yards, and training activities necessary to the support of the operating forces.

Let us first turn our attention to the operating forces. To understand their purpose and function, it may be helpful for us to step back for a moment and take a long view of the role played by the sea in the international affairs of today.

Over the centuries we have developed a civilization in which trade and travel among the various nations of the world are a necessary part of our existence. The percentage of international trade which is borne upon the sea is overwhelmingly large; the sea is the great common of this planet, and its only tolls are skill and determination. It is the use of the sea for transportation and trade between nations that lies at the root of the usefulness of the Navy to the United States. The traditional mission of the Navy is to insure that the United States has the use of the seas for such purposes as her national interests may require.

The actual implementation of sea power is an expensive and difficult matter. Only a few nations of the Free World are economically able to maintain significant navies; it is left, in effect, for the United States and its maritime allies to perform the task.

Such a situation is not new to world history. Indeed, the United States itself owes much of its own opportunity to grow to maturity undisturbed by disruption of sea trade to the control of the world seas exercised by Great Britain's Navy during the nineteenth century.

Maintaining control of the seas for international trade is only a small part of the story, however. Just as commerce travels the highways of the world's oceans, so can the implements of military power. The Navy's amphibious forces stand ready to transport highly trained assault troops to beaches around the world where they can land against opposition if required. The logistic support ships of the Navy carry tanks, ammunition, fuel, and food to the land and air forces of our unified commanders throughout the world.

Perhaps most important, the sea can act as a launching platform for our strategic deterrents. Our aircraft carriers can send their planes deep into the land masses of the world with a variety of weapons; our Polaris submarines conceal virtually invulnerable launching pads from which weapons of great power can strike any portion of the world.

In sum, the Navy is fundamentally involved in maintaining a peaceful and quiet regime upon the oceans of the world but, at the same time, it stands ready to unleash a wide spectrum of military force from the sea if required for the safety of the United States.

Evidence that this force is dedicated to the interests of the Free World is provided by a network of treaty agreements. We are committed to nations in every corner of the Free World by treaty: NATO links us with fourteen; the Rio Treaty with twenty; SEATO with seven, ANZUS with two; and bilateral agreements with Japan, South Korea, the Philippines, and Taiwan China complete a picture of international involvement that is important to every U.S. citizen. Each of these arrangements is a solemn commitment on the part of the United States that could require the use of armed force. In some of these places, we have troops and supplies on the spot, but in most we rely on the great power of modern transportation to move force in quickly if needed. Both the Air Force and the Navy would be deeply involved in moving Army and Marine troops to far-distant places if trouble should occur.

The presence of American forces in troubled spots of the world can have a tangible effect; such forces are at once the symbol and the substance of American policy. This point was made forcibly for me during a recent visit to Hong Kong.

I was attending a reception at the home of the American Consul General, high on one of the wooded mountains that overlook the picturesque harbor. I had spent the day wandering through the shops of this exotic and prosperous free city that maintains itself at the end of a peninsula extending from mainland China.

Almost as though to flout the regimented and drab society that dominates the mainland, Hong Kong exhibits an extraordinarily free and open way of life. Although the overcrowding of the city by mainland refugees makes some grim poverty and deprivation inevitable, the overall impression of prosperity, ebullience, and affluence is strong. The visitor to Hong Kong must inevitably feel that he has arrived at a gay and exciting place—a sort of Oriental combination of Paris and Rio.

Reflecting on what I had seen during the day, I stood on the open porch of the Consul General's home, looking down into the harbor from the elevation of a thousand feet or so. We were on the island of Hong Kong proper and could look northward across the harbor onto the peninsula of Kowloon, where an even larger portion of the city is located. It was dusk and the lights of the city were blinking on, illuminating the dim outlines of the land masses.

One of the British civil servants who administer the Crown Colony of Hong Kong stood beside me and pointed out the places of interest that were visible from where we stood. Far below, the Star Ferry chuffed back and forth on its endless task of transporting people between the two parts of the city.

"It's an amazing balancing act," I said, "to maintain this rich city in such a location."

"Well, of course, there are sound economic reasons why it goes on," said my British friend, referring to the foreign exchange advantage that Hong Kong provides mainland China, "but there's more to it than that."

The Englishman puffed on his pipe for a few moments and said nothing. Then he added, "I've worked out here for years and don't pretend to understand it. However, one thing I am sure of." Using his pipe for a pointer, he motioned toward the center of the harbor. There, outlined with strings of white lights, loomed the hull of a massive-looking United States aircraft carrier. Anchored around her like watchdogs were four lean, gray destroyers. The Star Ferry, the colorful junks, the tugboats—all the other traffic of the harbor—were dwarfed by the carrier. "Down there," he went on, "is one of the things that holds this show together today." There were few places one could go in this bustling city of 3 million people where this clear evidence of the power and determination of the United States could not be seen.

Anchored there in the calm, tropical moonlight of this exotic city, the carrier was striking physical evidence of a national policy backed by strength.

The carrier in Hong Kong harbor was at the end of the long chain of organizational and training effort which is required to place effective ships and planes of the Navy around the world.

Organizing and training the 900 or so active ships and 7000 operating aircraft of the Navy is a task of major proportions. To start with, virtually all of the ships and planes, along with their crews, are assigned either to the Pacific or Atlantic Fleets, which, in turn, are part of the unified Pacific or Atlantic Commands. Both the Atlantic and Pacific Fleets maintain two numbered fleets: the Second and Sixth in the Atlantic, and the First and Seventh in the Pacific.

In effect, the First and Second Fleets act as mother organizations from which units are periodically detached for deployment to the Sixth (Mediterranean) and Seventh (Western Pacific) Fleets. These deployments last from four and a half to seven months and represent the most active period for the ships involved.

In addition to the numbered fleet organizations, which are mainly for operational purposes, the Atlantic and Pacific Fleets maintain type organizations (destroyers, submarines, amphibious ships and so on) which are responsible for the maintenance, training, and other support of their ships. Thus, while a ship is in the period between deployments to the Sixth or Seventh Fleets, it will undergo repairs and training by its type commander.

Operations with the First and Second Fleets are usually based on the West and East Coasts, respectively, and are generally of a slower pace than those with the deployed fleets.

Each ship and group of aircraft undergoes a training cycle which prepares it to take part in its scheduled deployment. This training cycle, which lasts about two and a half years for a ship, occupies the period between shipyard overhauls. Immediately after an overhaul, which may last for three months or longer, a ship will undergo a period of elementary training to insure that the crew is ready for safe operation at sea. This over, the ship will report to the training command of the respective fleet for a refresher course in its particular missions—an exception are the submarines, which are trained by their own type commander. This period of advanced operational training may be followed by operations with the First or Second Fleet or with the antisubmarine forces. Six months or so after the completion of overhaul, the ship is ready for deployment to the Sixth or Seventh Fleet as the case may be.

About 60 per cent of a deployment period is spent in exercises and other operations at sea, usually of a fairly complex and advanced nature. The remainder is spent in making visits to the nations which surround the normal operating areas of the two deployed fleets. A Sixth or Seventh Fleet deployment represents the top of the training cycle for a Navy ship or aircraft squadron, and is a rich experience for all concerned. No one enjoys the long absence from home, but the satisfaction that comes from being part of a well-trained team that knows it can do its job if called upon is a large reward in itself.

The return from deployment usually results in a month of leave and recreation while the ship remains moored in her home port. Rest period over, the ship will return to operations, usually based in its own home port on the East or West Coast. These operations, once again, may be with a type commander, the First or Second Fleets, or with the antisubmarine forces. It is customary to detach sizable numbers of a ship's crew upon return from deployment, and these operations may have to start at a slow pace as new crew members are broken in to their new tasks. As operations pick up, another deployment will be scheduled, and upon return from it the ship will usually be ready for another visit to the shipyard for overhaul.

General descriptions of schedules don't convey much of the flavor and tang of the actual experience, however. Let's see if we can't do better by going aboard one of the Navy's big amphibious ships for part of her deployment to the Mediterranean. . . .

Norfolk, the amphibious base at Little Creek, and home are just memories as our ship plows its way steadily eastward across the Atlantic toward Gibraltar. The hard work of training, of loading the ship for the deployment, of making last-minute arrangements, of farewells to families—all of these lie behind us now as we are actually underway for the Mediterranean and nearly six months of hard work away from home.

Our ship is a large one, built to carry troops, helicopters, and several of the large craft used in landing across the beaches. Displacing about 10,000 tons, it is capable of speeds up to 20 knots and is built so that it can flood down in the water to facilitate the launching of the amphibious craft held in the large drydock-like cavity that occupies most of the after part of the ship.

We have about 300 Marines on board in addition to our crew of more than 200 men. Our ship, called an LSD, is only one of several highly specialized types necessary to conduct a modern amphibious landing. Since we are equipped with good facilities for a staff, we have on board with us the Marine officer who commands all of the Marines in our task group.

Upon departure from Norfolk, our particular group of ships was designated a *task group*, given a specific identifying number, and placed under the naval officer whose primary assignment is to command a squadron of amphibious ships, under the amphibious type commander of the Atlantic Fleet. Our task group will shift from the Second Fleet and report to the Sixth Fleet commander shortly after we pass through the Straits of Gibraltar. The Sixth Fleet commander may assign our group to one task force within his Fleet for a period of time and then later assign us to another. When our period of deployment is over, the commander of the Sixth Fleet will sail us for Norfolk with orders to *chop* (change operational command) back to the Second Fleet as we leave the Mediterranean.

Right now, however, our thoughts are focused on the large amphibious exercise which is scheduled to take place on the southeastern coast of Spain not long after our arrival in the Mediterranean. This is to be a major effort. Aircraft carriers will supply high-performance jet fighters to provide air superiority over the beachhead; cruisers will supply shore bombardment (simulated) to precede the landing; helicopter carriers will provide fighting helicopters to drop Marines inland behind the beachhead; and every type of amphibious ship will be involved in putting Marines, tanks, trucks, jeeps, guns, supplies, and ammunition ashore over the beaches. Planning for the exercise has been going on for more than a year, and it will provide the opportunity to test new concepts which have been evolved in the Marine–Navy teamwork characteristic of our amphibious forces.

The days at sea while crossing the Atlantic are quiet ones. The Marines are gathered in groups, going over the detailed plans for the landing; the ship itself conducts drills for gun crews, damage-control teams, and for such casualties as can be simulated without interfering with our eastward progress. Training movies are shown, and the many new members of the crew begin to learn their shipboard tasks. Our crew will remain relatively stable during the six-month deployment, but since we can expect to lose large numbers of them when we return to the United States, it is imperative that every training opportunity be taken during the months ahead.

Finally, the always-exciting morning of landfall is at hand and we have the experience of seeing Gibraltar loom over the horizon, silhouetted by the rising sun behind it. The Mediterranean is at hand; new ports, new experiences, and hard work lie ahead.

The weeks before the big landing exercise pass in a blur of preliminary rehearsals in which the beach is approached but no troops put ashore, of short periods in port, of storms at sea, and just plain hard work in getting all of our equipment ready for the main show.

In due time, the great day arrives, and we have a front seat from which to watch one of the most complex of all modern military operations. All through the night our LSD steams in company with the other amphibious ships, steadily approaching the carefully designated position from which we will launch our helicopters and landing craft. Volumes of operation orders spell out in detail what each unit is expected to do. The beach itself acts as the reference point, and from it arcs, rectangles, and squares delineate the various sea areas reserved for each necessary activity. The helicopters have certain paths which they must follow; each ship which will send landing craft to the beach must insure that they are launched in such a way that they can follow the proper lanes at the proper time; each of the ships must unload in a definite sequence to be sure that the proper equipment arrives on the beaches at the proper time.

Supervising it all is a Navy admiral, embarked in a large communication ship built especially for the purpose. He is in command of the entire operation—including the land fighting—until such time as the Marine general in command of the troops feels he is well enough established ashore to take command of the beachhead. The transition is a delicate one and requires much preliminary planning.

Although we have studied the operation plans and understand the concept behind what we see, the overall impression from the bridge of the LSD is one of confusion. Jet fighters scream over the beach at enormous speeds, strafing and bombing; helicopters seem to fill the air in all directions; some landing craft go directly to the beach to discharge their men and cargoes, others employ long floating ramps over which they unload from a distance; the sea area near the beach is filled with ships of every size and description.

The beach itself is the scene of tremendous activity. The simulated opposition soldiers retreat stubbornly as more and more troops and supplies come ashore from our landing craft. Tanks, self-propelled guns, and armored troop carriers add to our fighting force as they roll up the sandy beach. Teams with radios and other special equipment establish themselves ashore to direct the fire from the supporting ships and aircraft. The whole effect is one of organized, noisy confusion.

As we watch from the bridge of our ship we cannot but be impressed with this example of the way the sea can be used to exert the military force of our nation in a limited war situation. Such an effort could be used in a variety of locations throughout the world to bring American strength to bear if it were necessary in the pursuit of our policy. No nation in the world today can match our skill and experience at this particular brand of warfare.

The major landing exercise over, we enjoy a week in port in Genoa. The exciting cities of northern Italy are all close at hand, and while some of us visit museums, others seek out more exciting and active pastimes. It is worth pointing out in passing, however, that the crews of the Sixth Fleet ships are very much aware of their position as American representatives in the Mediterranean and, by and large, the conduct of these men ashore is exemplary. There are always a few whose improper conduct penalizes the many, but it is no exaggeration to state that, for the most part, the behavior of the Sixth Fleet crews is a source of justifiable pride both to the Navy and to the United States.

Our deployment extends over the Christmas holiday period, and those fortunate wives who can find the airplane fare and have either no children or children old enough to bring along join the ships for the period. Italy, Greece, the south of France, and Spain all offer appealing opportunities for leave and travel, and another experience is added to our growing list.

A few more operations with the Fleet ensue, and the time for return to the States has arrived. Gibraltar falls behind and once more we settle into the routine of an Atlantic crossing. Our task group has not changed in composition, and the same ships that left Norfolk what seems like a very long time ago return together.

Home is the sailor—with a sense of satisfaction at having increased both professional and personal experience. Many of the crew of our LSD are detached, along with several of the officers. A period of repair, of quiet, of retraining, and of more modest operations begins. But the pace will gradually increase until, within a year, the time will come once more to leave the shores of Virginia and set sail for another deployment—this time to the Caribbean. The changing pace of such a cycle, often repeated, brings to mind the words of another place and time . . .

To every thing there is a season,
And a time to every purpose under heaven:

A time to plant, and a time to pluck up that which is planted;
A time to break down, and a time to build up;

A time to cast away stones, and a time to gather stones together;
A time to rend and a time to sew . . .

A time of war and a time of peace.

The aircraft carrier of the Seventh Fleet anchored in Hong Kong and the LSD discharging landing craft off the coasts of Spain are only two examples of the Navy at work. Large and well-equipped task forces organized for antisubmarine warfare roam both the Atlantic and Pacific, ceaselessly seeking new ways to improve their capacity in what may be the most difficult of all modern Navy tasks. Highly-trained crews take their nuclear-powered Polaris submarines on quiet patrol in the Norwegian Sea as well as the far reaches of the Pacific. Doughty little minesweepers ply their dangerous trade in wooden ships constructed to avoid triggering the magnetic mine. Patient oilers, refrigerator ships, and ammunition ships follow their paths back and forth across the oceans, supplying their seagoing sisters with the sinews of war. And occasionally one sees the sleek nuclear-powered surface ships, harbingers of a new era in Navy history.

And yet all of this is only the seagoing arm of the Navy. While it is true that the ships at sea are the pride and symbol of the Navy, they are by no means the end of "what the Navy does." Behind them are the repair bases, the training schools, the supply depots, the bureaus in Washington, the Navy Department itself.

What does the Navy do? It takes some 900 ships, 7000 planes, nearly 700,000 men and women, and organizes them into an effective manifestation of American strength upon the sea—dedicated to maintaining the freedom, prosperity, and peace of the Free World.

It is a mission worthy of our best.

CHAPTER THREE

What Do Naval Officers Do?

In our first two chapters we have discussed the Navy and some of its tasks in broad terms. Clearly, a young man contemplating a career as a naval officer would like to know more concretely just how all of this will affect him. If he became a naval officer, what sort of activity would he have from day to day? What kind of life would he have on board ship? Where and how would he live in the ship? What, in short, could he expect in his first years of duty as an officer?

Let's begin our attempt to find answers to these questions by taking a short cruise on one of the Navy's new destroyers. . . .

It is early morning as we stand on the dock waiting for the boat that will take us out to the anchored destroyer we can see dimly through the mist. The nip of October is in the air and we stamp our feet lightly as we wait. There is almost no wind and it looks as though we'll have a beautiful day when the sun burns the Newport morning mist away.

Before long, a small, hooded, gray boat appears, headed our way from the anchored ship. With a jingle of bells, it pulls up to the dock. A young sailor jumps out to tend the lines and we step on board, soon finding our places in comfortable black leather seats under the hood covering the forward part of the boat. The mist begins to clear during our short ride and the sun is just beginning to peek over the horizon as we walk up the small, wooden ladder rigged on the side of the destroyer. It takes us up to the main deck, where we find a young officer wearing a dark blue overcoat with the shiny new single stripe of an ensign. He returns our salute as we, following tradition, request permission to come on board.

A young messenger shows us to the wardroom, a sort of combination dining room, club, lounge, and conference room for the ship's officers. It is a comfortable-looking place, perhaps the size of an ordinary living room, equipped with a long table and a few leather-upholstered easy chairs and sofas. A reproduction of Winslow Homer's "Eight Bells," with its salty-looking men engaged in the reading of a sextant during a storm at sea, hangs in a prominent spot. There is a well-stocked bookshelf and a few magazines are in evidence. The captain is finishing his breakfast at the head of the long table; the other officers are conspicuous by their absence—apparently busy readying the ship to get underway. The captain rises, greets us, and asks if we'll have breakfast or a cup of coffee. We settle for coffee and it is soon brought by a white-jacketed steward, who is one of the ship's company assigned the duty of taking care of the wardroom and its functions.

"Well, you two ought to see some pretty good antisubmarine work this week," the captain says as we drink our coffee. "One of the nuclear-powered submarines from New London will meet us south of Block Island and we'll have a few days to see what our new sonar equipment can do with him."

"Will we be able to go down to the sonar room and watch your men at work?" we ask.

"Sure thing—I'll make certain there's someone with you who can explain what's going on; it can look pretty mystifying if you don't have a few pointers."

Now a lean, red-haired lieutenant commander steps into the wardroom and says, "Excuse me, Captain, the ship is ready for getting underway." It is the executive officer.

"Thank you, Mr. Harrison. Will you two come up to the bridge with me and watch us get underway?" the captain asks.

A short climb up two steep, metal ladders brings us to the bridge of the destroyer. From this vantage point, we can see most of the topside, both forward and aft. Some of the crew are lined up at quarters, preparatory to standing out of the harbor. Others are securing the gangway ladder, which has now been brought on board, while still others busy themselves with the anchor, which is apparently being hoisted in.

An efficient-looking lieutenant who is wearing binoculars and seems in charge, turns to the captain as we reach the bridge and reports, "Anchors at short stay, Captain."

"Heave 'round and heave up," he replies, and in a short time the ancient cry "Anchor's aweigh, sir," rings up from the forecastle. The lieutenant officer of the deck orders the engines ahead one-third and gives the helmsman a course to head for the channel. Slowly, almost imperceptibly at first, the lean, gray ship begins to move. "Anchor's in sight—clear anchor," calls out the forecastle a moment later. Shortly, the anchor is housed.

This done, the officer of the deck orders ahead two-thirds, and the destroyer begins to pick up speed. The shoreline is slipping by rapidly; there is still not the slightest feeling of vibration or strain as the powerful ship loafs along through the harbor's calm water. It is clear that the lieutenant officer of the deck is handling everything; he is giving all the orders as we clear the harbor. The captain, however, keeps a watchful eye on his actions as well as on the work of the navigators, who carefully plot and replot the position of the ship as it proceeds toward the sea.

Rounding the rock-lined entrance to Newport harbor, we turn our bow toward the open Atlantic, and a slight but unmistakable motion can be felt as the ship responds to the Atlantic swell. The motion produces a mild feeling of exhilaration today—but also an awareness that it could produce quite a different sensation on a stormier day.

Brenton Reefs Lightship slides off to port, and on the starboard bow we can see the dim outlines of Block Island; the broad Atlantic lies ahead. The colorful signal flags that have shown our international call as we cleared the harbor are snapped down and the ship's loudspeaker calls out: "Now hear this! Secure the special sea and anchor detail; set the regular underway watch."

With this word, the extra men stationed on the bridge, on lookout, and other key positions during the process of clearing the harbor begin to leave their posts, and the members of the regular morning watch section take over. Speed is increased again and soon we are flashing through the bright sea at well over

20 knots. Spray flies up from the bow, and even though there is little actual wind on the ocean this morning, a sharp breeze of salt air strikes our faces as we stand on the wing of the open bridge.

"Right tangent, Block, 265! Left tangent, 257!" sings out a tanned and leathery sailor standing near us as he sights through his compass repeater and reads the bearings on Block Island to the west. We glide past it southward on our way to deeper water and our rendezvous with the submarine. Somewhere, over to the westward, our opponent for the week to come is also southward bound; but, gliding beneath the surface of the sea, he is unseen. Briefly, we think he is missing a glorious morning and some wonderful fresh air, cooped up down there in his hermetically sealed environment. Well—each to his own taste.

We have to run some 50 miles south of Block Island and off the continental shelf before we can find the deep water that we will need to conduct meaningful exercises with our nuclear-powered playmate from New London. Thus it will be some time before we are ready to begin. In the meantime, the captain suggests a brief tour of the ship. He sends for Ensign Collins who, it turns out, is the young officer who greeted us at the gangway when we came on board early in the morning.

As we follow Collins down the metal ladders and away from the bridge we chat a bit and learn that he is a graduate of the NROTC unit at Ohio State University. He has been on board since July and is an assistant to the engineer officer. When he is qualified in this department, probably about Christmas time, he expects to become the communications officer; he also hopes to become qualified as an officer of the deck not long after that.

Our first stop is in the Combat Information Center, or CIC, a dimly lighted space where a huge plotting table dominates the middle of a large compartment. It is surrounded by radar repeaters, vertical plotting boards, teletypes, voice radios, and a host of other complex electronic equipment which combine to provide the captain with the basic information he needs to fight his ship in battle. Edge-lighted vertical sheets of plastic stamped with compass roses enable the CIC men to plot friendly and enemy ships and nearby land masses with grease pencils, which show up vividly in the dim lighting. Collins describes the procedures used by his ship to cope with attacks by enemy aircraft. He explains briefly the complex electronic equipment which tracks these incoming raids, as they are called, instantly computes their course and speed, and transmits the necessary information to the long, thin, Tartar missiles which we had earlier seen hanging menacingly from their sleek rack on the deck aft.

At present, however, things are relatively quiet in the CIC. The radar screen shows the pear-shaped mass of Block Island off to the northwest and a few slow-moving merchant ships to the south and east. These are being carefully plotted with grease pencils to determine their point of closest approach to our track; from time to time, this information is reported to the bridge. Each merchantman is given an arbitrary letter designation to identify him; we hear a CIC man report: "Skunk Bravo tracking as before, CPA still 080 at 5200 yards, range now 14,000. Do you have him in sight?"

"That's affirmative; looks like an oiler," the bridge replies. This exchange of information helps the CIC men to keep their log of contacts accurately—a record which has proven valuable on many occasions when questions arise as to just where a merchant ship was at a certain time.

Leaving the CIC, we make our way down into the crew's mess and galley area. The dining area is empty now, but its bright colors and sparkling clean atmosphere look inviting. Its tables are covered with plastic and edged with stainless steel, raised to keep the food from sliding onto the deck in rough weather. Collins explains that the crew serves itself cafeteria-style onto compartmented metal trays which will hold an entire meal. The tables are built to accommodate four men apiece, and comfortable padded seats with small backs are provided.

Collins goes on to say that a great deal of effort is being expended to make destroyer messes more pleasant places to eat without losing the basically efficient man-of-war atmosphere that has always characterized these fighting units of the Navy. Collins mentions that he, personally, does not think the metal trays are the right answer.

"When you get hot potatoes and gravy spilling over into your salad and ice cream, your enthusiasm for this one-tray business begins to wane," he explains, and goes on to say that the Navy is experimenting with a return to individual dishes, accepting the fact that it will entail a lot more dishwashing and breakage. We can't help reflecting, as we walk into the galley, that this detailed interest in just how the crew is eating, on the part of a young officer not even connected with the ship's supply or commissary department, is a good sign. Officers genuinely interested in the welfare of their men usually have a good ship.

The galley is deep in the preparation of the noon meal, which we note, with some lack of enthusiasm, is stew. The long, slow motion of the ship underway is not so exhilarating now that we are below decks and not exposed to the cool fresh air of the bridge.

On our way to the engine room we pass a small compartment where a crew member is getting a haircut amid fairly conventional barbershop surroundings, albeit a bit cramped. Going down more of the inevitable steel ladders, we pass the supply compartments, which hold the thousands upon thousands of repair parts required to keep this ship and its machinery operating. Storekeepers check out parts to crew members, keeping careful records showing what has been issued. In due time, this information is reported to higher authority to establish Navy-wide usage records; these in their turn enable the supply activities to provide the fleet with the right amounts of the right spares in the right places. Collins reminds us that nothing can immobilize a modern fighting ship faster than the lack of a needed spare part for some basic piece of equipment. The day when the spare part could be manufactured on board by an ingenious crewman is fast disappearing—parts for computers and teletypes are just not turned out by hand.

The engine room is a vast, confusing array of dials, valves, insulated pipes, switchboards, cables, and huge pieces of machinery. But Collins explains that there is a system in all this apparent disorder. He starts with the turbines which drive the two main propeller shafts, shows us where the steam lines enter these turbines after their trip from the boilers located in other compartments, shows us how the spent steam finds its way into huge sea-water-cooled condensers under the turbines and is pumped back to the fire rooms to be once more turned into energy-laden steam.

When he explains that all of the other equipment in the compartment is peripheral to this basic arrangement, merely providing lubricating oil, electrical power, fresh water, or other needed services, we begin to understand the overall scheme of the way the ship is driven. We can't help being impressed, in passing, with our young guide's familiarity with this machinery. It is only a few months ago that he left his midwestern university; obviously Collins has not been wasting his time since July.

When we return to the wardroom after our tour of the ship, we find it transformed. The stewards have spread the white cloth for lunch, and the gleam of silver and china give an altogether different look to the room. About a dozen of the ship's officers have assembled, and they are gathered in small groups, talking, or reading magazines. One group pores over the morning sports pages and discusses yesterday's football scores.

Finally, the captain comes down from the bridge, and we are ready to sit down. Although we can contain our enthusiasm for food, it is a good lunch, and the salad seems particularly appetizing. The meal is nicely served by the stewards. After the dessert, when the coffee is brought on, the captain explains a little of the program for the week. "We'll be working with the nuke from now until Thursday noon. We'll conduct elementary exercises at first and then work up to something more complex, where the submarine is not restricted in speed or depth. Fortunately, the nukes can work around the clock so we can get our elementary sonar work off at night, leaving the day for the battle-stations men."

We reply that we don't exactly understand what he means.

"Well," the captain explains, "with about 250 men and 20 officers on board, our ship's company is constantly changing. We have new men to train all the time, and the sonar operators are no exception. There is a small group, the first team, which we call our battle-station operators. These are the men who would operate the gear in real combat, and they are the ones who can handle our nuclear friend from New London when he really begins to step out and use all his capabilities. However, we have many others we want to train up as replacements, and they have to learn to walk before they can run. Some of them, in fact, have never even seen the gear operate against a real submarine. Now, here in this deep water–it's over 1000 fathoms–the SSN can operate under us at a safe depth–say, 200 feet–all night long and give these boys a chance to send out pings and watch them echo from the submarine in all sorts of conditions and ranges. The submarine will remain at constant depth, at low speed, and take whatever courses we ask him to. Then, next morning, our battle-station men are rested and ready to go into something more difficult. See how it goes?"

At this point, the intercom from the bridge informs the captain that the SSN is in the area, communicating with us on the underwater telephone, and that we hold him on the sonar equipment at a range of about half a mile. The submarine reports he is ready to go to work.

"These modern rendezvous are really something." The captain laughs. "We used to meet the diesel subs out here and at least get a look at them before they submerged. Now they make the trip out here submerged, call us on the underwater telephone, and get to work without so much as putting a periscope out of the water!"

The captain excuses himself to go to the bridge, but not before asking Ensign Collins to take us down to sonar control for a look at the afternoon's work.

Down metal ladders we go, this time into a smaller compartment containing a long console of gray, electronic-equipment cabinets. Each is covered with switches, dials, and cathode-ray screens. The light is dim and the equipment is manned by about half a dozen alert-looking young men in blue dungarees. "These are the battle-station men," Collins whispers, as we walk over to the largest of the ghostly green cathode screens.

The sound of the sonar room is like nothing we have ever heard before. As the huge transducer under the hull of the destroyer pulses and sends its charge of energy streaming out into the sea, a corresponding ring of electrons fans across the face of the sonar screen, slowly spreading like the ripples on a quiet pond.

The noise of the sonar instrument is a quavering, searching, almost plaintive note until, in the quiet spread of its ripples, it is interrupted; and then, seemingly without delay, we hear a distinct *plink* as the echo returns to us. The probing fingers of sound have found the steel hull of the submarine in the depths of the sea.

The cathode-ray screen reveals a bright green spot where the submarine lies, enabling the operators to measure the direction and distance of the enemy. Again and again the whining note of the sound beam ripples out into the water; each time the metallic *plink* reveals the location of the submarine.

"That all there is to it?" we ask Collins.

"Well, don't forget that under the rules we're using this week, the submarine isn't allowed to shoot back." Our guide grins. "Also, wait until the sub begins to crank on some speed and maneuver around a little."

Gradually, as the afternoon wears on, the submarine begins to put on more and more speed and to turn more suddenly. The water becomes confused with his wakes and the knuckles left by his rapid turning. More than once we see the operators concentrating furiously on a bright green spot, clearly the submarine, only to find, suddenly, another submarine indication, just as clear, several thousand yards away. Which is real? Which false? Methodically, without concern or panic, the sonarmen go about their work, applying the various tricks of their trade to enable them to tell which is the submarine, which merely a disturbance in the water that reflects the pulsing sound waves of the sonar with confusing regularity.

On occasion, the submarine is simply lost—nowhere to be seen on the screen. Then contact has to be reestablished by means of the ever-useful underwater telephone, which enables us to talk to the submarine officer of the deck almost as clearly as we could talk to our own bridge on the destroyer's intercom equipment.

"Come on up topside; we're getting ready to do something pretty interesting," Collins says. When we break out into the bright sunlight, open blue sky, and brisk air, it is as though we have entered a different world. For a moment we forget about antisubmarine warfare, sonars, and underwater telephones, and just drink in the beauty and stimulation of the scene. A glance, however, at the blue seas rolling by the side of the ship reminds us that lurking not far beneath is one of the twentieth century's most modern weapons of war—and we are here to learn how to deal with it, not to absorb the beauties of the fall afternoon.

Collins points to the extreme after portion of the ship. There, on a small platform, a small helicopter whirls its blades in the sunshine, readying for flight. As we walk aft to get closer to the platform, Collins shouts, "How do you like that pilot?"

Closer examination fails to reveal even a trace of one, and it is not until Collins explains that we realize this is a radio-controlled drone helicopter, designed to deliver weapons against the submarine at considerable distances from the destroyer. While Collins is explaining, the motor of the drone increases its tempo, and before long the helicopter is airborne and on its way to the location of the submarine as reported by the sonar.

Swiftly, without hesitation, the unmanned helicopter flies to its mark, guided by an officer who works with a small set of controls placed so that he can easily see the drone in flight. When it is in the correct location the officer gives a signal and a small shape drops from the framework of the aircraft into the water—a submarine-seeking torpedo.

"There goes the fish—now let's hope it gets him," Collins says. "Let's go back to sonar. That will be the best place to find out how we did."

Not long after our arrival in the sonar room, the underwater telephone blurts out a quick message from the submarine: "Bingo! It got us—we heard it hit the hull in the engineering spaces."

"Roger—good news. Take a breather while we recover the fish," replies our sonar officer.

"Wilco. You can plot me on course south at 3 knots; I'll hold until I hear from you again or until 1800, when I'll come to periscope depth and give you my position by radio."

Before long the destroyer is at the scene of the drop looking for the torpedo, which is constructed to come to the surface and float motionless after its practice hit. One of the lookouts finally sights it, a few hundred yards from the plotted position reported by the CIC.

Soon a boat is lowered and on its way to recover the practice torpedo. It is easy to sense the feeling of satisfaction experienced by almost everyone on board about the torpedo hit. The unceasing competition between destroyer and submarine changes in nature from time to time, with first one, then the other appearing to have the advantage, but its basic nature remains the same: the denizen of the deep against the more open-handed warrior of the surface. Each group has its own proud traditions, each is working toward a common ultimate goal—the security of the United States.

The remainder of the week is more of the same, with the submarine and the destroyer continuing their endless minuet—sometimes slowly, while the beginners go through their paces, then rapidly and skillfully when experienced hands take over. We lose our queasiness about the motion of the ship, and the meals served in the wardroom three times a day begin to look better and better. All too soon Thursday noon rolls around and our submarine, whom we have gotten to know quite well through the medium of the underwater telephone, requests permission to terminate the exercises and proceed independently.

"With your permission, I'll clear the area on course 160 at 18 knots, depth 300. My destination is Bermuda," comes a voice from the submarine, a new voice that we have not heard all week. Sensing that the submarine captain is speaking, our captain picks up his telephone microphone on the destroyer bridge and answers: "Permission granted. Thank you for an excellent three days of work. We've learned a lot."

"Thanks. We enjoyed working with you, and the learning worked both ways," the submarine replies.

"Have a good weekend in Bermuda."

"Wilco," comes the final message from the submarine as he begins to fade into the distance at high speed.

It is only when we come up from the sonar room for the last time that we realize we have never seen our submarine companion. We have worked with him for three days, twenty-four hours a day, almost always in sonar contact, never more than temporarily out of touch by underwater telephone. We have even gotten to know the voices of the different officers of the deck on the underwater telephone. We felt a little as though we were losing an acquaintance when he departed, and yet we have never seen one shred of evidence of his presence—not even so much as a periscope or a swirl of disturbed water.

Only by the electronic evidence of the instruments in the sonar room did we know that our lively companion was not merely a figment of our imagination.

But, wait, there was one other proof! A careful look at our recovered practice torpedo reveals a smudge of submarine black on its yellow-painted nose. . . .

In their more than sixty years of service to the Navy, the destroyers have earned an enviable place. Perhaps more than any other element in the Navy, the destroyermen carry on the American seagoing traditions of ruggedness, resourcefulness, enthusiasm, and hard work. Whatever the task, be it knocking down airplanes, hunting out submarines, bombarding the shore before amphibious landings, acting as far-flung pickets for the fleet, or simply showing the American flag in a troubled spot of the world, the destroyers can do the job.

A young officer seeking his first assignment at sea can scarcely find a better place to learn than in a destroyer. Small enough to give him early responsibility, large enough to go anyplace and do almost anything, a destroyer is, in the words of Admiral Arleigh Burke, himself one of the Navy's great destroyermen, ". . . the roughest, toughest training school the Navy offers."

And, many might add, the best.

Not every new officer will be fortunate enough to serve his first sea duty in destroyers, but the general policy of the Bureau of Naval Personnel is to order new line officers to at least one tour of duty (usually two years) in destroyers within the first four years of commissioned service if at all possible. As for the other two-year tour, there are, of course, many other surface-ship assignments: cruisers, aircraft carriers, amphibious-warfare ships, mine-warfare ships, and fleet auxiliaries such as oilers, ammunition ships, refrigerator ships, and repair ships.

At the end of four years, the new officer will probably be assigned to shore duty. Depending upon his requests and needs, this may be postgraduate education at the Navy's Monterey, California, school or at one of the nation's leading universities. On the other hand, it may be instructor duty at the Naval Academy or one of the NROTC units established at more than fifty colleges and universities throughout the country. Assignment to a shore staff or to one of the technical bureaus or staffs in Washington is also a possibility.

These first shore assignments provide an opportunity for the young officer to improve his understanding of the Navy, its work, and its structure. They provide opportunities for learning the staff, educational, or administrative functions of the Navy against a background of concrete knowledge of what the Navy does in its ships at sea. This point is particularly important; a young naval officer coming to a shore assignment from sea duty brings with him a store of useful background information—information which not only makes the tour of shore duty more valuable to him, but also enables him to make a genuine contribution to the command to which he has been assigned.

In the Navy of today, it is necessary to assign a certain number of newly commissioned officers directly to shore commands. This is unfortunate for all concerned; as someone observed long ago, N-A-V-Y spells ocean, and it is only through day-to-day participation in shipboard life at sea that the new officer can absorb the meaning and flavor of his profession. In short, the right place for the newly commissioned officer is at sea.

Not all line officers will want to remain with—or even embark upon—a career devoted only to the surface ships of the Navy, sufficient as it is to a full and varied life within the service. One of the largest and most important subdivisions of the line is that of aviation; it comprises more than 40 per cent of all the unrestricted line officers in the Navy today. The carriers of the Navy represent a vital segment of its actual striking power, and the business of exercising control of the air above the seas is one of the Navy's most important and exciting functions.

Naval air is a demanding business. The task of flying high-performance jet aircraft on and off the weaving decks of aircraft carriers during day and night operations is among the most difficult of modern aviation tasks. It requires the best in coordination, training, skill, and self-confidence. However, for those who can meet its challenges, naval aviation has been—and remains—a highly rewarding branch of the naval profession.

Although his early years are heavily saturated with operational experience, the naval aviator is far more than simply a highly trained and specialized airplane pilot. He remains fundamentally a line naval officer, and as his career advances, his opportunities for command at sea become richer. Command of the Navy's aircraft carriers is reserved exclusively for naval aviators of long experience and high professional competence. The command of fleets and task forces very often falls to aviation flag officers because of their backgrounds with the flight operations that make up so much of the day-to-day business of a task force at sea.

How does a young officer embark upon such a career? Some apply for flight training after obtaining an ensign's commission in the Navy; others enter into flight training from a noncommissioned status.

About 850 commissioned officers enter flight training annually at Pensacola, Florida, headquarters for the Navy's Air Training Command. At one time it was the custom for officers to have one or two years of sea duty in surface ships before applying for flight training, and this procedure still has many advantages for both the officer and the service. However, the majority of commissioned officers commencing their flight training today are ensigns with very little or no sea experience.

A second large group of prospective aviators are called Aviation Officer Candidates. These are young men with college degrees who may enter from civilian life or from the enlisted ranks of the Navy. After a four-month officer candidate course at Pensacola, they are commissioned ensigns in the Naval Reserve and finish their eighteen months of flight training in this status.

There is one other path to naval aviation, through the Naval Aviation Cadet Program. This program is open to civilians who have completed two years of college and to enlisted men in the Navy, who may enter the program with less advanced educational requirements. These young men conduct fourteen of their eighteen months of flight training as Aviation Cadets; they are then commissioned ensigns in the Naval Reserve and complete their flight training in that status.

However, whether commissioned officer, Aviation Officer Candidate, or Naval Aviation Cadet, all undergo very much the same course of training in naval aviation itself. If you were to choose one of these three paths, let's take a look at just where you would be and what you'd be doing during those eighteen busy months.

The Naval Air Station at Pensacola is a huge, modern, and complex assembly of training and repair facilities. Its 5500 acres include such diverse installations as shops for major overhaul and repair of fleet aircraft, headquarters for several large naval aviation commands, and the home base of the Navy's famed Blue Angels. However, the part of Pensacola which will concern you upon arrival is a graceful-looking three-story red brick building of colonial style with palatial white columns in front.

Don't let its country-club appearance fool you. This is the Indoctrination Building, and for those of you who enter naval aviation as AOCS or Aviation Cadets coming from civilian life, this building will introduce you to military life with a bang. Civilian haircuts, civilian clothes, and the casual posture and attitude of your life beforehand will take swift departure here as you undergo the first ten days of Pre-Flight known to Pensacola veterans as Indoc. It's rough but it's not without a purpose.

You are entering upon a serious business where meticulous attention to detail, a completely no-nonsense attitude, and the habits of military discipline and thoroughness are important not only to prevent the loss of a very expensive airplane but also—and more important to both Pensacola and you—to prevent you from killing yourself while learning to fly. Naval aviation has no room for the young man who thinks that *perhaps* he would like to be a naval aviator. You must be determined, dedicated, and competent. Indoc is a first crack at finding out how determined you are and, in the process, giving you some introduction to what it means to be in naval aviation.

Indoc is the first small portion of a sixteen-week course known as Pre-Flight. During this course, the students never get into an airplane, nor do they focus particularly upon the basics of flying one. Just as Indoc attempted to guide you toward that sense of self-discipline which you will need in the months ahead, so the remainder of the Pre-Flight course attempts to introduce you to the mental disciplines you will need.

Math and physics are the backbone of a course which touches on mechanics, hydraulics, heat transmission, electricity, and metallurgy as well as elementary physiology, navigation, and general naval orientation. If you have had engineering work in college, it will prove of great value, but there is nothing in the Pre-Flight course which requires more than a good high school education, an alert mind, and the willingness to work hard.

And work hard you must. Reveille comes at 5:15, the first class is at 7, and a two-hour enforced evening study period is followed by taps at 9:30. By the time you complete Pre-Flight, you will have attended about 450 classroom hours of instruction and participated in physical activities ranging from a rigorous athletic program to a survival course at a nearby U.S. Air Force base in which, for three days, you will be on your own in a near-tropical wilderness, making use of your previously gained knowledge of how to trap small animals, recognize edible plants, and defend yourself against your environment. Don't expect much time off; you'll have some weekends, but you should count on spending literally all your time on the base, at school, or in the barracks. It's not meant to be easy or pleasant.

The officers who enter flight training in commissioned status go through a shortened (about six-week) version of the Pre-Flight course with fewer restrictions, for they have had at least part of its content in other locations. However, they cover enough to enable them, at the end of the sixteen-week period, to start the actual business of learning to fly on approximately equal footing with the other two groups.

Pre-Flight over, you will leave the barracks that has been your home for sixteen weeks and move to nearby Saufley Field, where you will begin to learn the anatomy and characteristics of the little orange-colored T-34 Mentor, which will be the first naval aircraft you will master. By the time you are ready for your first flight you will know—at least theoretically—how to fly the Mentor.

You will make all the required preliminary checks on your plane, but you will make them under the careful eye of your instructor, who is interested for several reasons—not the least of which is that he will accompany you on your flight. When you are satisfied that all is in readiness, you will climb into the front of this two-seated craft, and your instructor will get into the rear, where he has controls exactly matching yours. After checking out your radio with the control tower you will attempt to start the engine. You've done all this in a trainer beforehand, but still, the actual pushing of all the necessary buttons and switches in the correct sequence can become a problem when you know it's for real. However, finally the engine will cough, sputter, pour out clouds of white smoke, then clear its throat and settle into that steady purr of power that lets you know you have a ready and reliable engine.

When the plane captain on the ground nearby gives you the thumbs-up signal indicating that everything is right, and you have permission from the control tower, your instructor will taxi the Mentor out to the end of the runway. He'll run the engine up to the required manifold pressure, you'll help him make the other necessary checks, and in a moment you'll be roaring down the runway waiting for that delicate moment when the stubby wings of your Mentor can lift you off the ground.

Once airborne, your instructor will let you handle the controls yourself for awhile to begin to get the feel of this training airplane. Approaching the landing runway, you'll watch intently as your instructor brings the little Mentor in for the landing. The first flight over, things begin to move rapidly. You'll be handling the controls a little more each day until, at the end of about eleven flights, you'll be ready for a pre-solo checkout by an instructor other than the one you've been flying with each day.

This instructor will let you do the whole job: takeoff, maneuvers in flight, and landing. If he gives you a thumbs-up rating, your thirteenth flight will be solo (probably to prove that superstition has no place in the modern Navy!).

Since the earliest days of aviation, the first solo flight has had a special status all its own. It's not hard to see why. You have been learning a delicate and dangerous task at the hands of a skilled and experienced man. He has been with you during your every flight, ready to back you up with a word of warning or, if need be, to actually take over the controls. Maybe you've never really needed him, but his presence there in the rear cockpit has made a deep psychological difference. Now, you're going to do it alone. It's only one of a long series of challenges that naval aviation will present to you, but to most men it is one of the most memorable.

After soloing, you'll get about ten more flights, some solo and some dual, to check you out on elementary acrobatics, flying in company with other aircraft, and more difficult types of landings. Eight weeks will complete the primary flight training. At this point, you will be faced with one of the many crossroads in your career in naval aviation: jets or propeller airplanes? There are good arguments for both, one of which is bound to be your own personal preference.

Let's assume you choose jets. You'll go to an altogether different naval air field (probably outside of Florida) for a twenty-week course in the T-2A Buckeye trainer jet. You'll spend about half of each day flying and the remaining time in the classroom. Upon completion of your basic jet training, you'll return to Pensacola for gunnery training and—highly important—to become carrier qualified.

You'll start out with three dual flights in which you'll land at a specially prepared strip laid out ashore to resemble a carrier deck in shape and size. The next ten flights are solos in which you must demonstrate the ability to make a perfect simulated carrier landing on dry land. Once past this hurdle, you will fly out to sea to rendezvous with Pensacola's own private aircraft carrier, the *Lexington*. Coming down toward this postage-stamp landing target as it weaves its way through a wrinkled blue sea is usually the challenge that naval aviators remember most vividly after their first solo.

The same mirror at the side of the landing target which helped you in the field landings is there: if the ball in the mirror is too low, you're too low. Too high—you're too high. Keep that ball in the center; watch your flying speed. Closer and closer comes the stern of the carrier. All of a sudden you feel your wheels hit the deck. Acting on your instructions, you hit the throttle and scream off the deck; only touch-and-go, that was what they wanted. Looked pretty good.

Another touch-and-go is followed by your first arrested landing. This time you will approach with your tail hook down, and when you hit the deck, you will shove the throttle forward just as though you were making another touch-and-go. Your engine will put out its usual throaty scream of power, but this time you go nowhere. One of a set of arresting wires at the stern of the carrier has caught your tailhook and you are firmly stopped on the flight deck. The simulation of the touch-and-go is, of course, a safety feature, as it will prevent a missed arresting cable (or a broken one) from causing a tragic accident in which the plane rolls along the deck and into the water, vainly attempting to get up power and flying speed to take off again.

Six successful arrested landings earn you the designation *carrier qualified* and you are well on your way to becoming a full-fledged naval aviator. You will be transferred again (don't plan on staying put during flight training) to another locality—possibly Corpus Christi, Texas—for advanced jet training. Here you will fly hotter airplanes, such as the supersonic F-11 Tiger, receive training in high-altitude and high-speed gunnery and the use of air-to-air missiles like the Sidewinder.

Those pilots who have chosen propeller planes or helicopters follow basically similar paths of instruction—different, of course, in details—as they develop from fledgling fliers into pilots qualified to operate the high-performance weapon systems of today's fleet aviation. In about eighteen months, the group of young men who started out as greenhorns at Indoc in Pensacola will be officers in the Navy, qualified naval aviators, wearers of the golden wings, and members of one of the proudest flying fraternities anywhere in the world.

About 1700 men complete this training every year: approximately half of them are officers to begin with, the other half are divided between Aviation Cadets (NavCads) and Aviation Officer Candidates (AOCS). This group of some 850 ensigns received through flight training each year constitutes a significant number of new officers for the Navy and the Marine Corps (whose aviators are trained in the same manner). In fact, when the 900 or so Aviation Observers (non-pilots who, nevertheless, may serve in flying billets such as navigator or engineer in multiengined land-based aircraft) trained annually at Pensacola are added to the new pilots, the Naval Air Training Command at Pensacola is found to be the second largest annual supplier of new officers for the Navy, surpassed only by the Officer Candidate School at Newport.

Different as are the lives of the naval aviator and the surface ship officer, they both meet the basic definition of the unrestricted line officer—qualified to command at sea. The third important group in the Navy's unrestricted line consists of the submariners.

The submarine, as an instrument of war, has had a wavering and erratic history. The concept of a ship which could proceed beneath the surface of the sea, thus using it for concealment and protection, is an old one. The story of Bushnell's *Turtle*, which failed in its attempt to screw an explosive device into the hull of an anchored British man-of-war during the American Revolution, has become familiar to every schoolchild. Napoleon toyed with a submersible built by Robert Fulton and rejected it. The American Confederacy lost several crews in its often-salvaged *Hunley* before it finally made a kill, blowing itself to final destruction in the process.

At the beginning of World War I the submarine was still considered a somewhat comic-opera character in the naval scene, which was dominated at that time by the battleship and the armored cruiser. However, an incident occurred at the very outset of that conflict which sounded the warning bell of more serious things to come. . . .

It was the morning of one of those beautiful September days at sea, on which not a cloud mars the sky, only a puff of breeze ripples the surface of the sea, and the sole reminder of the storm which has passed is a long, rolling swell. An observer would have seen nothing but the empty sea—unless he had very sharp eyes. In that case, he might have noticed a dull black metal tube the size of a man's arm rising vertically out of the water, leaving behind a wake of white water as it moved.

If the sharp-eyed observer had looked out to the horizon he might also have seen the object of the periscope's attention: the faint outlines of the upper works of a warship. Relentlessly, like the eye of a cobra, the periscope watched the approaching ship. Occasionally the black tube disappeared from sight, but soon it would rise again and watch, always leaving its small, splashing, white wake.

Before long, another warship came into sight astern of the first, and then still another. The three gray ships moved with ease and grace, their long bows knifing into the swells and then rising to shake themselves free of the water as though they were alive. If there was excitement at the other end of the periscope, it did not show in the unblinking stare with which it measured the movement of the three gray ships. It simply watched, watched . . . until, finally, a swirl of churning water could be seen near the periscope. A few seconds later a faint line of white bubbles ran swiftly toward the leading ship. The bubbles headed for a point in the ship's intended track. Straight as a die they stretched across the dark blue water.

When the torpedo and the ship met their rendezvous, a sharp crack ran through the water like the sound of a hammer striking a steel plate. A fraction of a second later came a dull roar that seemed to grow in magnitude as it reverberated through the sea. A column of water shot up the side of the warship and rose high above its deck. It seemed to hang frozen for a moment like a white marble monument before it melted back into the surface of the sea. The great ship slowed, her course wavering uncertainly to one side. Before long she was stopped, her stern settling into the sea. Steam blew wildly from her smoke pipes.

The sinister black tube appeared again and carefully appraised its handiwork. As the second ship stood by to take survivors from the first, two more lines of bubbles, stretching like taut strings diverging from a common origin, headed out from the periscope.

Two more sharp cracks were followed by dull roars, and the second cruiser began to sink. Again the black tube broke the surface and stared while the third cruiser stood by her two stricken sisters—waiting, almost like a lamb for the sacrifice.

Two more torpedoes streaked for the remaining ship. Vainly she tried to maneuver to avoid their racing white lines of bubbles, but one struck and she too was crippled. A few minutes later still another torpedo appeared and the debacle was nearly finished. The third ship turned on her side; her crew scrambled down her sides as she turned, and for a few desperate moments they stood on her flat red keel as she hung on the surface. Then a sudden plunge and she was gone.

Within a short time, the dark waters had closed over three of Great Britain's most powerful warships, leaving only wreckage and a few small boats to mark the tragedy.

The tiny submarine, unscratched, surfaced and chugged off toward the cover of the Dutch coast to charge its storage batteries.

Thus, in September of 1914, the submarine introduced itself to serious naval warfare by sinking the British armored cruisers *Aboukir*, *Cressy*, and *Hogue*. Depth charges were unheard of, and the mighty guns of the British ships, which could have blown the fragile U-boat out of the water had they caught it on the surface, were reduced to firing futilely at floating wreckage which they thought resembled a periscope.

Although the U-boat made a deep impact upon the conduct of World War I, the U.S. Navy submarine saw little action during this conflict. It was in the wide-ranging conflicts of the Pacific war with Japan that American submarines left their mark and carved a meaningful place for themselves in the U.S. Navy.

The development of the nuclear-powered submarine, only a decade after the close of World War II, and the subsequent introduction of the Polaris submarine have moved this still small segment of the Navy into increased prominence. About 2000 officers and 20,000 men today man the approximately 150 submarines in the active fleet. Command of these ships is given to officers of a variety of ranks and lengths of service. Junior lieutenant commanders skipper the diesel-powered fleet submarines, while command of the Polaris-firing nuclear-powered submarines is sometimes held by junior captains.

Although there are good reasons why a two-year tour of duty in destroyers or other surface ships is a sound investment of time for the prospective submariner, the fact is that many of today's submarine officers enter their training immediately after commissioning as ensigns. The submarine service does not offer a program comparable to those of naval aviation, where a young man can learn his specialty and earn an officer's commission at the same time; submarine officer training accepts only commissioned officers at the present time.

Today's submarine force is undergoing a major transition from diesel to nuclear power. This change is a fundamental one for several reasons: first of all, the submarine officer is deeply involved with the mechanical plant of his ship, regardless of the department in which he actually serves. An old custom requiring each man on board to know every part of the submarine as thoroughly as possible persists into the far more complex ships of today. Secondly, the difference between a diesel-powered submarine and one with nuclear power is more than simply the fact that a different set of machinery is located in the engine room. The entire ship is different, more complex, built to accomplish different tasks, and requiring different skills.

To gain some idea of what is involved, let's take another cruise. This time, let me describe an experience I had not long ago, visiting one of our new Polaris submarines on its initial sea trials. . . .

The chill breeze of a New England April morning blew onto the docks from across the river as I walked toward the waiting ship. The wooden piers, arranged like semaphore arms branching from one master wharf that jutted out into the deep river, were alive with activity.

A hundred workmen went in different directions, while bright yellow cranes chugged busily up and down about their business, their peanut whistles shrilly piercing the air. Trucks, laden with materials, beeped impatiently for the cranes to move out of their way. A small green tug tooted and careened recklessly around the end of a pier.

Moored alongside the docks were the submarines, their hulls variously painted, depending on their stage of construction; some were a brilliant orange, some a dull ochre, and one, looking ominous and sleek in the busy surroundings, completely black. The bustle of activity around this ship, as well as her new paint, indicated something special was about to happen here.

As I stepped on board I was greeted by the captain, an old friend. He was casual and friendly as usual, but his face showed just a trace of expectancy and pleasure at finally getting his ship to sea. On the deck, clusters of white-sneakered sailors stood by the lines which moored the nuclear ship to the pier. We walked to the bridge and I stepped out on one of the diving planes that jut from either side of the sail structure, supporting it. There I could observe what went on without being in the way. Temporary lifelines rigged around the edges of the sailplanes indicated this sort of sightseeing had gone on before.

From my perch I could easily see the captain as he glanced at his watch and looked at the river to see what traffic might affect his getting underway. Suddenly the loudspeaker near us crackled: "Bridge, executive officer, the ship is ready for getting underway in all respects."

The captain leaned over and spoke quietly into the intercom, "Maneuvering, bridge, stand by to answer bells." Checking astern once more, he called down to the deck, "Take in two, three, and four. Heave around on one."

The mooring lines were quickly taken on board; the bow line was led to a drum-shaped bronze capstan and wound around it. In a moment the bow of the submarine began to swing toward the dock while the stern pivoted away.

"Avast heaving, take in one," went the order from the bridge. Then, with one more careful look at the river, "Back one-third."

The propulsion plant of the big submarine had been operating and undergoing tests all through the night. From the reactor itself, where pressurized water silently flowed past uranium-laden fuel plates to carry heat to giant boilers that generated steam for the turbines, through the engine room, where whirring turbine-generators spun out their electrical power to breathe life into this floating city, all was in readiness. Although I could not see them, I knew a score of highly trained officers and men were watching every detail.

At the captain's command, the main throttle was opened, the huge bronze propeller began to bite the water, and the ship backed slowly into the river. The captain put her rudder over and the stern swung ponderously upstream to point her bow for the open sea. After another terse order from the bridge the engines changed direction, and as the propeller kicked ahead, the river water bucked and swirled at the stern of the ship. Gradually the submarine gathered headway and the docks of the shipyard began to fade in the distance.

The mooring lines were stowed and the men cleared from the main deck. As speed was built up, water began to slide up on the blimp-shaped bow and across the deck where, minutes before, men had been working with the lines. As the submarine nosed out into the open sea, speed was increased again, and water now boiled across much of the forward part of the ship, racing under the sailplane where I stood. The sea breeze, accentuated by our speed, struck with pleasant firmness against my face.

A few hours later we were in water deep enough for diving to test depth. In the meantime we had rendezvoused with the submarine rescue vessel, a small, tuglike ship that would escort us through our first dives. By now I had deserted my post on the sailplane and come down via a long vertical steel ladder to the control room of the submarine. I found myself in a compartment about the size of a small living room which was crowded with people, dials, instruments, valves, and machinery. Like the cockpit of a modern jetliner, the control room of a modern submarine looks to the uninitiated like a hopeless jumble. But in both cases, a logical pattern is involved, and once one learns to sort out the functions of the various groups of instruments, an understandable picture begins to emerge.

On the periscope stand, a small raised platform overlooking most of the control room, stood the captain. Even though the submarine was still on the surface a periscope was raised, and the khaki-shirted skipper stood with one arm draped over a handle while he studied the relative position and course of the rescue vessel.

Satisfied, he looked away from the eyepiece and, turning to a gray metal box nearby, lifted a microphone. "How do you read me?" he asked.

"Loud and clear. How me?" answered the rescue vessel, perhaps a mile away at the time. The answer came over a speaker which could be heard in the general vicinity of the periscope stand.

"Same," the captain replied.

The skipper then outlined his plans to the rescue vessel. He gave his intended course and speed and indicated that he would drop down to test depth by stages, checking out over the underwater telephone at each pause.

Next the skipper turned to the diving officer, standing a few feet from the periscope stand. "Ready to go?" he asked. The diving officer nodded.

The captain leaned over to a different microphone suspended nearby. "We'll be going down shortly for the initial submergence; we will use pressure." The captain's brief message was heard in every compartment of the ship. Although pre-warning is not a normal procedure, the captain thought it advisable on this occasion to let everyone know, especially since the unusual procedure of bleeding air into the ship was to be used to make a final check that the hull of the ship was tight and that no opening had gone unobserved during the yard work.

The roar of high-pressure air filled the control room as the diving officer watched the barometer needle swing upward. The officer's left hand was spread wide as he watched; finally he clenched his fist, signaling to the man operating the air valve that he was satisfied. The roaring stopped as suddenly as it had begun. The diving officer watched the barometer needle closely for nearly a minute.

"Pressure's holding, Captain," he said finally.

"Sound the diving alarm," the captain replied.

A raucous honk echoed twice through every corner of the

ship. The periscope was lowered. Small toggle switches were moved on the control panel near the periscope stand. Lights flicked to indicate valves opening. The muffled roar of rushing water filled the control center as the ballast tanks began to flood. As the ship began to settle slowly in the water, the engines kept her moving forward at about 5 knots. The diving officer leaned over the backs of two leather-upholstered seats in which sat the men operating the diving planes. The stern planes are important in the early stages of the dive, and attention was focused on their indicator. The sailplanes (on which I had been standing when we got underway) do not come into play until the ship is deeper in the water.

The planesmen were using control sticks much like those found on multiengined airplanes: partial steering wheels mounted on the end of a post hinged to swing forward and aft. The fore-and-aft motion controls the planes while either steering wheel controls the rudder.

Everything seemed to be going smoothly when suddenly the ship began to nose down sharply; the depth gage began to spin. A sudden tension caught the room. Had someone made a mistake in the ballasting calculations? Was she going down too fast?

"Hard rise on the stern planes," said the diving officer. Slowly but surely the angle eased back to normal. One could almost feel the room relax. The submarine seemed to snuggle into the sea nicely after her little caprice.

"Shut all vents," said the diving officer.

The switches flicked, the lights changed.

"Make your depth 65 feet," ordered the skipper.

"Make it 65 feet, aye, aye," repeated the diving officer. Slowly the ship leveled out at periscope depth and then began to sink slowly below it.

"Pump two thousand from forward trim to sea," the diving officer said. Again the toggle switches flicked, a pump whirred, and the submarine was lightened as a ton of sea water was pumped from one of the internal tanks used to balance the ship. Obediently, she climbed back to her ordered depth.

"Up periscope," said the skipper to an assistant standing with him on the platform. Another lever was thrown and with a swish of hydraulic oil the shiny metal tube of the periscope started upward from its well in the platform.

When it reached full height, the captain grasped the handles and walked it slowly around. The bright sun flashed across the sea at almost the top of his periscope. Occasionally, a wave would obscure his vision as it splashed over the lens, but visibility was good and he could see the rescue vessel plodding along about a mile to starboard. He glanced quickly at the diving officer; the depth was right on its ordered value. He was beginning to feel better; his ship was finally acting like a submarine after all these months tied to a dock.

Swinging the periscope again toward the rescue vessel, he grasped the microphone of the underwater phone. "At periscope depth and everything fine," he stated.

"Looked like a mighty nice dive, Captain," the rescue vessel replied.

"Going to 200 feet now; let you know when we're there," the captain said.

"Roger," came the acknowledgment.

The captain ordered the new depth and the deck of the control center again slanted forward as the big submarine nosed deeper into its element. Bystanders instinctively reached for something to hold, looking like subway straphangers as the angle increased even more. As the ship approached 200 feet, the angle slowly eased off and she slid into her new depth gracefully and easily. Here a careful check was made throughout the ship for leaks, while the rescue vessel was again informed of our progress over the underwater phone. Leaks can range from a few drops coming through a loose valve to things like a broken pipe that can, of course, mean real trouble. Many pieces of machinery within the submarine use a constant flow of sea water for cooling while the ship is submerged, and thus not only the hull of the ship but also much internal piping must withstand the pressure of the sea.

Within a few minutes, the captain was ordering a new and lower depth; the ship was being taken down step by step, being checked at each new depth to see that she was responding properly. At each stop the rescue vessel was reassured over the underwater phone that all was well. At each new stop, various pieces of machinery were operated to see that the crushing weight of water was not distorting the hull in such a way as to inhibit any vital functions. Occasionally, the ship would lurch and sway as slugs of water were expelled forcibly from the torpedo tubes to check the workability of their firing mechanisms at the new depth.

Finally when the ship was at her maximum designed depth and the captain was satisfied in all respects, he again turned to the underwater phone.

"I'm at test depth and everything is fine. Will be moving out for full-power tests now; you may return to port. Thank you for your excellent services today," he said.

"Roger, returning to port," came the reply, muffled and wavery now as it reached us through many layers of water.

The skipper ordered the speed increased and the ship brought to a more moderate depth. The course was changed to due south, and I could feel the ship bank and quiver as she responded to the new commands. We were taking to the sea by ourselves.*

I walked aft to the engineering spaces, which would now become the focus of attention. En route I passed through the compartments where the firing of the Polaris missiles is controlled, and the compartment containing the huge, vertical launching tubes. Empty now, they were only a promise of the power the ship could eventually exert.

Stepping into the engine compartment, I was in a different world. Almost as clean as a hospital room, with its stainless steel, white paint, copper tubing, and shiny gages, the engine room breathed an air of efficiency and power. The distinctive smell of hot oil pervaded the room as much as the incessant whine and throb of its turbines. I stepped into a small enclosure leading off the main engine room. There a half-dozen men scanned a set of instruments that would put even a jet aircraft layout to shame.

Literally hundreds of dials, gages, and meters reported on every aspect of the nuclear power plant. Neutron flux, steam pres-

* I have described the test-dive procedure used prior to the loss of the *Thresher*. Subsequently, some procedural changes have been instituted as additional precautions.

sure, flow rates, liquid levels, temperatures, salinity levels, and countless other variables were displayed in this nerve center.

A rather intense young man, khaki shirt open at the neck, stood with his back leaning gently against a fuze panel as he surveyed the instrument board. Arms folded, he let his eyes flick over the gages quickly as he made a few monosyllabic comments to the chief petty officer standing beside him. The khaki-suited officer was the chief engineer, and these trials were the culmination of long months of hard work in the shipyard for him. If he had been three men he could not have gone to all the required meetings, been all the places he was asked to go, and done all the things requested of him. Still, he had done his best, often at the expense of not going home for several days at a time. Now his power plant was ready, however, and he was getting the satisfaction of watching his hard work pay off.

Everyone on board knew that the big missile tubes amidships were the reason for the existence of this huge warship, with her tremendous concentration of modern machinery and technology. Inertial navigation, nuclear power, modern missile fire control, and a dozen other new developments had been combined to give her the capabilities she needed. But the missile testing would come later; right now the task was to prove the submarine's ability to dive deep and run fast. These were fundamental to her nature. The diving tests were over; now she would get her chance to run fast.

The engineer turned to an intercom speaker and spoke to the captain, far forward in the ship at the conning station by his now-lowered and useless periscopes. "We're all checked out back here and ready to commence the full-power tests when you are, sir."

"Start building her up," the skipper answered.

The 2-foot-wide steel throttle wheel was spun slowly to admit more steam to the turbines; the whine of machinery noise began to build up slowly in the background; the needle showing the power level of the nuclear reactor swung slowly higher.

Speed was increased to a designated value and held there until everything could be checked and the necessary data recorded. Just as in the process of going to test depth, stops had to be made along the way. Finally, the engineer gave the order to increase to flank speed, the Navy's term for full throttle. The wheel spun again. The whine of gears, the throb of pumps, and the hum of electric motors all blended into a full-throated sound of power. The submarine trembled like a straining animal. The reactor power needle hung near the 100 per cent mark. The ship's speed leveled out and the power plant seemed to settle back into a pulsing song of driving energy.

I felt the hair rise on the back of my neck despite the fact that I had gone through this experience before; it was almost impossible to think of the ship as an inanimate object; almost impossible to realize that all the power manifested around us came from a small metal core in the heart of the ship, surrendering the energy that had been stored in its atoms since time began.

The next day we were back in port. The trials were successfully completed, and I was leaving the ship. Her adventures, however, were just beginning. Soon she and her crew would be on their way to Cape Kennedy where they would fire practice shots on the Atlantic Missile Range. Later, they would depart for their patrol stations, where their missiles would join the rest of the Free World's ready defenses.

The task of building and operating the new fleet of U.S. Navy nuclear-powered Polaris and attack (torpedo-firing) submarines is a huge one which will be going on for some time. Like surface and aviation service in the Navy, it offers challenges, opportunities to learn, and excitement. How do you go about starting a submarine career?

There are at present three blocks of training available: first, the six-month Submarine School at New London, which is basic in nature; second, the year-long nuclear-power training course itself; and, third, the sixteen-week navigation and missile training course at Dam Neck, Virginia, which prepares officers to perform weapons-system duty on board the Polaris submarines.

These blocks of training can be combined in various sequences and not all submarine officers receive them all. Moreover, the submarine organization is now in a transitional phase, and changes are occurring regularly. Current directives from the Bureau of Naval Personnel provide up-to-date information on details.

Surface, submarine, and aviation—these are the three great divisions of the Navy's unrestricted line. There is more common ground among the three than one might suppose. All lead toward command at sea, all are actively concerned with the operation of ships, airplanes, and missiles in the sea environment, and all are primarily concerned with the use of the seas in furthering the national policies of the United States. Both naval aviators and submariners may attain command of surface ships such as tankers, attack transports, and underway supply ships. Submariners occasionally command cruisers, and all three groups intermingle in their assignments ashore.

Of the Navy's approximately 75,000 officers on active duty, about 48,000 of them are in the unrestricted line. Who are the others? Well, to begin with, about 10,000 of them are in the restricted line—officers who wear the star upon their sleeve but are not qualified to command at sea. Among them are the Navy's engineering specialists, those officers restricted to such duty as communications, law, or public information, and a rather large block (about 6000) of officers who have been promoted from enlisted rank for limited-duty assignments.

Most of the remaining 16,000 are in the staff: the various medical and dental services, the supply corps, the chaplain service, and the civil engineering corps.

There are, within the restricted line and the staff corps, a variety of interesting naval careers for the officer who, for reasons of physical condition or personal inclinations, does not aspire to command at sea.

Most of these careers follow more closely upon the civilian norm than upon anything peculiar to the Navy. The engineers, the lawyers, the doctors, the dentists, the nurses, the chaplains, and the civil engineers follow very closely the standards and daily duties of their callings in the civilian world. They do, of course, work within the Navy environment. Some, mainly the doctors, dentists, supply officers, and chaplains, are frequently members of ship's companies and share the seagoing experiences of the line.

However, naval officers outside the unrestricted line spend most of their careers in the naval shore establishment: its great hospitals, shipyards, bureaus, supply depots, research centers, bases, air stations, and manufacturing plants. They make an enormous contribution to the overall working of the Navy, and it could not exist without them. Many of them, particularly the doctors, work long hours for salaries that are significantly below what parallel effort would yield in the civilian economy. On the other hand, they have the advantages of a less hectic professional existence and of opportunities to do residence work and conduct research that would not be available to them outside the Navy. Many of the doctors have become interested in specialized fields such as submarine or aviation medicine, where they are able to make unique contributions.

The engineer specialists of the restricted line are the bearers of a distinguished heritage. There are only some 1500 such officers today, but though their corps is small, it has long had a tradition of high competence and great pride. These men are the modern-day counterparts of the naval engineers and naval constructors of the nineteenth-century Navy—the men who brought the steam-and-steel warship to reality by the turn of the century. Today, they are trained mainly at the Massachusetts Institute of Technology and provide the naval leadership in ship design, power-plant development, and aircraft innovation. Through the Bureaus of Ships and Weapons, they work with the various segments of American industry that build the ships, planes, and weapons for the fleet. On occasion they fill important material assignments on the staffs of the fleet commanders; only on very rare occasions are they part of an actual ship's company.

The life of the EDs or the AEDs (short for Engineering Duty Officer or Aviation Duty Engineering Officer) is a different one from that of the unrestricted line, but they spend their careers in close contact and cooperation with the men who will sail and fight the ships they develop for the fleet. Theirs is a more academic and intellectual task, and one that often appeals to young men who have an interest in engineering design.

Roughly half of the 16,000 or so staff officers of the Navy are associated in one way or another with the medical or dental services for the Navy. The next largest group (about 5500 officers) are those concerned with supply. These are the businessmen of the Navy, and their daily concern is with the efficient and timely provision of food, transportation, ammunition, building materials, fuel oil, gasoline, clothing, spare parts, and the countless thousands of other articles needed to keep the vast machinery of the Navy in motion.

Many of these officers receive graduate training at the Harvard School of Business Administration, and they have made many original contributions to the field of business management theory. Although they do not work in terms of profit and loss, they are concerned with the efficient operation of one of the world's largest businesses.

They are frequently on sea duty with the fleet, for most surface ships of destroyer size and larger have at least one supply officer on board. There they supervise such matters as the management of the commissary department, the pay of the crew, and the requisitioning of spare parts and other supplies.

The next largest staff group (about 1500) is that of the civil engineers, the base builders of the Navy. This is a very old corps, dating back to pre-Civil War days, and their task has traditionally been to build and maintain the docks and bases for the fleet. Recent organization changes have given them the responsibility for the construction and maintenance of all buildings belonging to the Navy, regardless of location.

The Civil Engineer Corps of the Navy has a proud tradition of professional excellence and leadership in the civil engineering field. Most of these men have received training at the Rensselaer Polytechnic Institute at Troy, New York. One of their proudest achievements, of course, was the development of the famed Sea-Bees (Construction Battalions) during World War II, which specialized in building airstrips and bases in unbelievably short times on newly occupied atolls in the South Pacific.

The smallest corps in the staff is that of the chaplains—about 1000. In addition to conducting church services wherever needed —on board ship or at naval bases—these men bring spiritual assistance and comfort to the men of the Navy in times of need. Many a ship's company has been made a richer and happier organization by virtue of the company of a good chaplain. Their contribution, like that of civilian clergy, is difficult to define in concrete terms. Suffice it to say that, to my knowledge, no experienced naval officer would like to see the Navy attempt to get along without its chaplains.

Whether a young man contemplating the Navy as a career should choose the staff over the line is a decision that he alone can make. Members of highly specialized professions such as medicine, law, or the ministry, know that if they enter the Navy it will almost surely be within the staff. Those who have engineering or business training could, conceivably, choose either staff or line.

A book such as this cannot hope to advise in such decisions. It can only take a quick and, I hope, objective look at the various opportunities in the Navy so that the decision need not be made entirely in darkness. My own prejudices are toward the line, but I have been in the Navy long enough to know that all branches of it are important and that the fleet needs the efforts of the staff to fight successfully just as much as it needs those of the line.

Staff, restricted line, and unrestricted line all offer an opportunity for a high order of service to country coupled with many deep personal satisfactions and rewards.

CHAPTER FOUR

How Are Naval Officers Educated?

What is the origin of the "special trust and confidence" that the government of the United States expresses in a new naval officer when he is commissioned? He has not performed any special services nor distinguished himself in action or otherwise. He is accorded the privileges of the officer group before he is ready to assume any but the most minor of its responsibilities. By what right does he claim such privilege in a democracy?

At the outset of an officer's career, the answer is education. By and large, the gold braid of the naval officer's commission is earned by formal education at the college level. The majority of the 75,000 officers of the Navy today possess baccalaureate degrees; practically all have had some college-level education.

Note the distinction here between training and education. The dictionary definitions of training emphasize such words as "discipline," "drill," "indoctrination," "good habit," and "sound practice." There is here the sense of learning how to do things, how to condition one's reflexes so that certain patterns of behavior emerge under certain circumstances. The destroyerman learning to distinguish the submarine from a false target with his sonar is being trained. The officer learning to fly is being trained, as is the submariner learning to dive his submarine. Military discipline is intensive training.

Education is a more elusive term to define. While it is true that discipline and drill may have their part here, too, especially in the early years of education, the essence of the concept is somewhere else. John Milton said: "I call therefore a complete and generous education that which fits a man to perform justly, skillfully and magnanimously all the offices both private and public of peace and war." Such a goal is too ambitious for most of us, but it is in this direction that the ideal is located. The very essence of education is its lack of boundaries; it goes everywhere and encompasses all things. But its ideal result is a man who can perform his tasks "justly, skillfully and magnanimously." Such goals cannot be attained by indoctrination.

It is hoped that the educated man has certain characteristics: he is open-minded, intrinsically fair, and attempts to seek out and learn those elements of his environment which are most admirable, most worthwhile, and most advantageous to the accomplishment of his goals. Ideally, he has respect for the truth and believes the objective search for this elusive concept is one of man's worthiest goals. He believes in the dignity and worth of individual men regardless of their station. The educated naval officer presumably understands the concept of nationhood in all its complexities, and has some grasp of his own role in the defense and expression of American nationhood.

There can, of course, be no guarantee that education, as such, will produce virtue and manliness—there is, indeed, no sure link between competence and conscience. But just as America, in the last analysis, depends upon the education of its people for its intrinsic strength, so the Navy depends upon education as a basic factor in the production of an officer corps worthy of the nation and its goals.

Perhaps Benjamin Disraeli expressed it for all of us when, speaking of his own nation, he said: "Upon the education of the people of this country, the fate of this country depends."

It was not always thus in the United States Navy. In 1805 the French Minister to Washington wrote an appraisal of American naval officers to his superiors in Paris. "The Americans," reported the Frenchman, "are today the boldest and most ignorant navigators in the universe."

There was considerable justification for both the praise and the criticism. Formal education had little part in the early history of the United States Navy. Boys were brought on board its warships in their early teens, designated midshipmen (because they lived and held a station somewhere between the officers in the after part of the ship and the crew in the forecastle), and then left to a combination of their own ambitions and the whims of their commanding officers.

It is true that some of the early captains took the task of training (and educating) their midshipmen more seriously than others. Thomus Truxtun (of *Constellation* fame), writing advice for his young men, hoped that each would ". . . while the dunces who are his officers or messmates are rattling the dice, roaring bad verse, hissing on the flute, or scraping discord from the fiddle, direct his attention to more noble studies which would sweeten the hour of relaxation."

We read that Oliver Hazard Perry, cruising in the Mediterranean, took special trouble to visit ports from which midshipmen could travel to the famed places of Greek and Roman civilization. Perry had a good library of his own on board ship, and both required and encouraged his midshipmen to read and broaden their education beyond the narrow requirements of navigation and gunnery. Perry apparently took a deep personal interest in the progress of his midshipmen and tried to maintain a competent teacher on board to teach them French and Spanish.

Unfortunately, commanding officers like Truxtun and Perry were in the minority, and most midshipmen grew up in environments that encouraged ignorance. With certain notable exceptions, naval officers at the beginning of the nineteenth century were more distinguished for boldness and good seamanship than for any pretension to education. Conduct ashore left much to be desired, and the young midshipmen in their eagerness to prove themselves men among men, all too often made the ancient mistake of confusing intemperance and rowdiness with manhood. They, in turn, influenced their successors along the same lines. It was becoming apparent to many thoughtful men, both in and out of the Navy, that the on-board system of educating the Navy's future officers left much to be desired.

Despite the fact that West Point had been founded in 1802, the Navy established no formal school ashore until the 1840s, when three events occurred which combined to precipitate reform.

The first event was the closest thing to a mutiny which has occurred in the U.S. Navy. In the fall of 1842, while the brig

Somers was returning to New York from the African coast, the captain was informed by one of the stewards that a mutiny was being organized by one of the midshipmen on board, one Philip Spencer.

Spencer, who happened to be the son of the then-Secretary of War, had already demonstrated a talent for getting into trouble. His antics had resulted in his dismissal from Union College in Schenectady, and doubtless his father hoped that the discipline of the Navy might accomplish what had not been done at home.

In any event, Midshipman Spencer was arrested and his personal effects searched. Among them was a mysterious paper, written in Greek. Another midshipman who could read Greek testified that it was a list of the crew divided into categories such as "certain" and "doubtful."

The captain immediately convened a court of inquiry from the officers of his ship and, after deliberating for a day and a half, they returned a report that Spencer and two enlisted men were guilty of a "determined intention to commit a mutiny," and further recommended that they be put to death. On the next day, with *Somers* still far at sea, the three men were hanged from the yardarm.

Upon the arrival of the *Somers* in New York, the story of the mutiny and subsequent hangings caused one of the great press sensations of the decade. The commanding officer of the *Somers* asked that a formal court of inquiry be convened to look into his conduct of the investigation and subsequent punishment. Although the court did meet, and found no fault, the entire affair was a nasty one. The senior Spencer attempted for years to have the captain tried in the civil courts for murder, and the resulting publicity focused public attention on the conditions in which future naval officers were being trained. It would be inaccurate to say that the *Somers* affair caused the establishment of the Naval Academy; but it would be naive to deny that it helped to spark the sentiment that led to action.

The second important event was the introduction of the steam-driven warship into the Navy. The launching of the *Fulton*, the Navy's first practical steam-driven warship, in 1837 was followed only a few years later by the Ericsson-designed screw-propelled

Princeton. It became apparent to many far-seeing naval officers that ships like the *Princeton* were going to revolutionize the Navy, and that the time had come for the midshipmen to have a school ashore in which to study the details of these new ships.

The third event was the arrival of the right man on the scene at the right time. In 1845, George Bancroft, a New England historian and schoolmaster, was appointed Secretary of the Navy by the newly inaugurated President, James K. Polk. Bancroft saw the need for an academy ashore, and skillfully navigated the political rocks and shoals which had blocked an academy before. In October of 1845, the school was opened at an old Army fort in Annapolis. The first students were about sixty somewhat confused midshipmen who were not at all sure that they would like this schoolboy-ashore arrangement. After all, they were used to being men of the world, as much at home in Port Said as in the Boston Navy Yard. They ranged in age from boys in their teens to men near thirty.

The first superintendent, Commander Franklin Buchanan, had a lively time trying to enforce some sort of military discipline. The midshipmen were quartered in the widely scattered buildings of the old Army post, and maintaining quiet during study hours and getting the lights out at taps were difficult tasks. Buchanan was always pleased to note, however, that one small cottage, appropriately named the Abbey, was never the source of a disturbance. No lights ever burned after hours, and soon Buchanan felt it no longer necessary to inspect the Abbey because of the exemplary conduct of its midshipmen.

He was somewhat depressed to learn later that the Abbey boys had dug a tunnel under the nearby wall and were simply spending their evenings in more congenial surroundings out in town, prudently dispatching a member to extinguish the lamps at taps.

Buchanan's successor, George Upshur, fell ill not long after he assumed his responsibilities, and he had an even more difficult time. One rainy night, after having been startled from his sleep by the thunderous discharge of a cannon in the Academy yard, Upshur assembled all the midshipmen and, in plaintive tones, reminded them of his illness and general physical weakness and of their thoughtlessness in arousing him from his much-needed sleep in the middle of a rainy night. He concluded: "I cannot govern you, young gentlemen, so if you will only govern yourselves, I will be delighted."

Needless to say, the rest of Upshur's tour contributed very little to the creation of order and discipline.

The Civil War seriously interrupted the development of the Academy, and it was only in the post–Civil War period under Admiral David Dixon Porter (of Vicksburg fame) that it began to acquire effectiveness as a military school. Porter knew the value of drill, routine, and tight internal organization in creating the intangible feeling of unity and coherence that characterizes a good military organization.

Porter was fortunate to have Stephen B. Luce, later to be founder of the U.S. Naval Institute and the Naval War College, as his second-in-command. During the Porter–Luce regime, organized athletics began to take the important place at Annapolis they have ever since held. New uniforms were obtained for the midshipmen, the band regularly played for military drill, and dress parades were introduced. Porter and Luce also introduced the system of gradual granting of privileges and authority through the four years of the course, as well as the system requiring upperclassmen to report the misdeeds of the younger students.

These concepts represented the Spartan side of the Spartan–Athenian balance which has characterized both West Point and Annapolis in their most productive years. There is every reason to believe that Luce wisely realized that overemphasizing the Spartan accent could be as harmful to the Naval Academy as neglecting it. Academic standards, particularly in engineering matters, steadily rose during this era of the Academy's history, with some of its graduates taking distinguished roles in American science, engineering, and industry.

The fortunes of the Naval Academy inevitably follow those of the Navy as a whole, and it is not surprising that the public interest in the Navy engendered by the writings of Mahan and the Navy's success in the Spanish–American War resulted in money for a new Naval Academy.

Congress appropriated a generous sum to rebuild the school on the old site, and work was started in 1899 on the gray granite buildings which have since become the very symbol of the Naval Academy. The architect was the famous Ernest Flagg, who took his inspiration from the International Exposition architecture of Paris. An even earlier French architectural influence is apparent in the chapel dome, which is almost a duplicate of that of Les Invalides. A massive dormitory was named Bancroft Hall, and a complex of recitation rooms and laboratories were named for Mahan, Maury, and Sampson. Fittingly, Admiral Dewey laid the cornerstone of the new chapel.

Smart new uniforms were introduced, and in 1907 "Anchors Aweigh" was played for the first time at an Army–Navy football game. And so, the traditions and physical setting that defined the Naval Academy until the beginning of World War II had been established by 1910. World War I did little more than ripple the continuity of the new spirit at Annapolis; by the late 1930s, not unassisted by Hollywood movies which spread its image throughout the world, the Navy's Academy for educating its officers had become a legend in its own time and a cherished part of the American scene and heritage.

In retrospect, the history of the Naval Academy can be divided into eras: pre–Civil War, when little was accomplished except starting; post–Civil War, when military discipline and routine were established; and 1900–1941, when the Academy matured and produced the great naval leaders of World War II. After the end of World War II, the Naval Academy entered a new period of transition.

Just as the introduction of the steam warship was instrumental in the founding of the Academy, so have technological changes influenced the academic revolution now underway at Annapolis. It is obvious that nuclear propulsion and the advent of long-range shipboard missiles with intricate fire-control mechanisms have placed a new order of requirements for technological competence on the naval officers of tomorrow. However, the reasons for the changes at the Academy are more profound and fundamental than simply the necessity to understand and operate new mechanisms.

The nuclear blasts over Hiroshima and Nagasaki ushered in

something more than just newer and bigger weapons of war. The advent of these devices, coupled with long-range missiles of great accuracy, brought a new dimension to warfare with which the military professionals, and indeed, the nations of the world, have yet to come wholly to grips. The concept of deterrence, while logical enough at first glance, has ramifications which simply do not yield to ordinary modes of thought.

The naval officer of the 1930s could exercise at sea with his ships, planes, and other weapons in the fairly certain knowledge that he was practicing for the kind of war that would be fought, if it should come. The officer of the 1960s, however, must grasp a vastly larger spectrum. The dimensions of naval war can now run from the all-out devastation of the Polaris submarine's mighty weapons, through the controlled but nevertheless powerful punch of a carrier–air-supported amphibious landing, down to the carefully restrained quasi-political efforts required to support a counter-insurgency operation ashore.

The new dimensions of warfare have had other effects. The Navy of today is many times the size of that maintained in the 1930s and far more diverse in nature. The Academy graduate of that era almost invariably went directly to a battleship, a cruiser, or a carrier to learn the facts of life in the fleet from the bottom up. In these ships the new ensigns underwent a careful course of training in the machinery and weapons (very much like those they had studied at the Academy) of their ships. Only after two years of such training were they permitted to apply for aviation or submarine training, or to transfer to a smaller ship such as a destroyer, where they might assume more direct responsibility. Indeed, they were even required to wait this two-year period before they had permission to marry.

Today's Academy graduate not only may marry upon graduation day—and many do—but he can look forward to a greatly increased range of possible assignments. He may go directly to flight training, directly to submarine training, directly to nuclear-propulsion training, or to almost any of the variety of surface ships possessed by the Navy. In all of these areas, responsibility comes much sooner than was the case prewar.

All of these changes—new weapons, new international implications of these weapons, a larger and more diverse fleet, nuclear propulsion, and much earlier assumption of responsibility—add up to a significantly different environment for the new officer. The Navy has realized for some time that this new environment required changes in the Academy curriculum but, understandably, has gone slowly in making them.

The old system, in which each midshipman took essentially the same course, regardless of previous education, was fundamentally aligned to the requirements of the pre–World War II era. It had, however, been enormously successful in the past, and the new direction in which to move was not altogether clear. Should the Academy simply attempt to teach more facts in four years, attempt to broaden its curriculum to embrace as many as possible of the diverse skills being required of its graduates? Or should it take an altogether different approach, changing from specific instruction in applied technology toward a more basic and fundamental education, hoping that its graduates would then be better prepared to handle the diversity of tasks they faced?

A question of philosophy was involved. The Navy was, as was the entire nation, aware of an increased need for more extensive education of its potential leaders. But if the Academy were to be simply turned into an institution of higher learning, could it continue the shaping and training of character which has been, through the years, one of its most valued attributes? The Navy realized that it had to strike a new balance between the Athenian and Spartan components at Annapolis. It had to be a balance which recognized the new requirements of the Navy but also satisfied the fundamental purpose of the Academy—to produce graduates dedicated to a career of naval service.

For many years, and particularly since 1959, the Academy has been making significant changes in its curriculum in an attempt to attain this proper new balance. Perhaps the best way to gain an idea of what is happening at Annapolis today is to make a short visit. . . .

The best way to see the Academy for the first time is to take the old Governor Ritchie Highway from Baltimore and park at the crest of the hill where the Academy first comes into view across the Severn River to the south. Its gray granite buildings rest on nearly 300 acres of flat land, much of it reclaimed from the river over the years to augment the size of the original Army fort. The green-hued copper roofs blend with the gray stone of Ernest Flagg's old buildings to create an air of permanence and solidarity. The waters of the Severn create a northern boundary, while the Chesapeake itself stretches out to the east. The tang of the sea surrounds the Academy, and the number of sloops and yawls which can be seen from a distance indicates that sailing has not been entirely replaced by power—not in this part of the Navy, at least.

Driving into the yard itself, we find a well-landscaped and beautifully maintained place. The yard is arranged around a central walkway which stretches from the massive dormitory, Bancroft Hall, to the main academic buildings. Halfway between, surveying the scene, is the gold-encrusted dome of the chapel. Monuments of naval history dot the yard and there is everywhere an atmosphere of quiet and dignity. Discipline and restraint are felt, rather than the easy informality of a college campus. The midshipmen who walk purposefully about have short haircuts, their caps are squarely placed on their heads, their shoes are shined, and their uniforms are neatly pressed and brushed.

All of this appears unchanged from the Academy of twenty-five years or more ago. Still, to the old graduate returning, there are easily noticed changes: when the signal for class sounds, there are no military formations marching across the yard to the measured beat of a lone drummer, each midshipman with slide rule in hand as though en route to battle (which, indeed, many of us felt we were). Now the call to class finds the midshipmen walking individually, talking freely about their studies as they find their ways to classes too diverse under the new curriculum to permit formation marching.

There are more changes than in the method of getting to classes, however. In attempting to broaden its intellectual scope, the Academy has proceeded along several different lines.

One of the most important innovations permits midshipmen who have completed college level (or advanced high school) work to obtain credit for such courses without taking them again at the

Academy. This is accomplished by a process called *validation*, in which entering midshipmen are examined in regular Academy curriculum subjects. If their marks are satisfactory, they are excused from the course and thus obtain time which can be used to take advantage of the second big change in the Academy curriculum, the elective courses.

The Academy now offers some eighty-five different electives, at least one in every academic department. Aerodynamics, Vector Analysis, Advanced Calculus, Topology, Organic Chemistry, and Nuclear Physics are examples of electives on the technical side of the curriculum. While these new courses are reasonably at home in a school which has always stressed engineering, such recent arrivals as Modern British Literature, Far Eastern Relations of the United States, the Economics of Labor Relations, and the Theory and Practice of Communism sound strange to the old alumnus reexamining his alma mater.

A third important innovation since 1959 is the grouping of these electives into academic minors and majors. At present, majors are offered in sixteen areas, including chemistry, physics, aerospace engineering, mechanical engineering, mathematics, foreign affairs, history, literature, and a foreign language.

There has been a continual increase in participation in the validation-elective-major program. In 1964, over 400 midshipmen were able to validate courses, and the graduating class of June, 1964 contained 152 men who had qualified for an academic major.

Electives and majors were not the only changes involved in the new look. The Academy decided to move ahead without delay in its de-emphasis of current technology and new accent on basic principles. No longer do the midshipmen study and make detailed sketches of specific naval boilers, pumps, and guns; courses in fluid mechanics, heat-transfer theory, and metallurgy have taken their place. Courses in theories of target interception and explosive damage have replaced drills on guns. Instruction on actual pieces of radar and sonar equipment is a thing of the past, and laboratory work on basic circuit analysis has arrived.

All of these new approaches emphasize mathematics, and as a result the work load, even without validation and electives, has gone up significantly. Leaving aside electives, today's midshipmen spend far more time per week on academic work than did their predecessors of only a few years ago. The basic curriculum, which devotes about half its hours to engineering and mathematics, about a quarter to the social sciences and humanities, and a quarter to professional naval subjects such as leadership, operations and analysis, and navigation, is a demanding workload by itself.

Clearly, the administration of such a complex curriculum requires an experienced hand. In the summer of 1964, the Academy appointed the first civilian Academic Dean in its history, Dr. A. Bernard Drought, former Dean of Engineering at Marquette University. Commencing with the class entering in the fall of 1964, the Academy is introducing still more changes in the curriculum designed to increase the time spent on social sciences and the humanities and further broaden the flexibility of the curriculum. In the past, electives were largely, though not entirely, restricted to midshipmen who could validate. Under this new program, 85 per cent of the total course will be taken by every midshipman, with the remaining 15 per cent of time available for electives. Thus every midshipman in the class of 1969 and subsequent classes will be able to obtain some concentration work—what might be termed an academic minor—in a field of his choice. Midshipmen who can validate should be able to complete a major with little difficulty, and some will be able to take courses which may later be accepted for graduate credit at other institutions.

There are other signs of academic ferment in addition to curriculum changes. The Academy has expanded its faculty, particularly on the civilian side. The summer of 1964 saw thirty-three new civilian members arriving, thirteen of them Ph.D.s. Including those active-duty officers who teach (mainly in professional naval subjects), over 70 per cent of the faculty hold master's or doctor's degrees.

A six-year $55 million building program has been launched, an important feature of which is Michelson Hall, a $13 million science building. On the less material side, there is growing evidence of an approach to academic matters which parallels that of civilian universities and colleges. For example, the Trident Scholar program, patterned on Yale's Scholar of the House concept, permits selected first-classmen (seniors) to pursue independent research supplemented by such regular curriculum and elective courses as they desire. Class attendance is not required of Trident Scholars, but monthly seminars with faculty advisers provide the necessary opportunities for advice and counsel.

Even the old Academy 4.0 marking system has gone with the new sweep of events. The stern old Indian statue, Tecumseh, so long the god of 2.5 (passing, under the 4.0 scale), is now, alas, only the god of the C, or perhaps the D under certain circumstances, as the Academy has shifted to the conventional civilian university grading system. No longer do instructors attempt to get a quiz mark every day so that class standings in each subject can be calculated to a whisker; the diverse curriculum makes it rather pointless now and, more important, the shift to teaching principles rather than detail makes the assignment of a monthly mark more appropriate than a daily grade.

With all of this increased emphasis on academic endeavor, it is only fair to ask what caliber students the Academy is actually attracting to undertake its courses. In 1964 and again in 1965, five midshipmen won Fulbright scholarships permitting them to study abroad after graduation; two officers from the class of 1962 were Rhodes Scholars, and a member of the class of 1965 has recently been selected for this honor.

The future looks even brighter, perhaps. A profile of the class which entered in the summer of 1964 (the graduating class of 1968) has a mean College Board score in verbal aptitude (verbal SAT) of 596, while the mean score in mathematical aptitude was 663. These scores compare favorably with most of the top colleges and universities in the nation today.

Of the 1200 or so members of the class of 1968, 79 per cent were admitted from public high schools, 21 per cent from independent schools. Seventy per cent stood in the top fifth of their secondary-school classes, ninety per cent in the top two-fifths. Eight per cent were either valedictorians or salutatorians and, perhaps most impressive of all, thirty-eight per cent were National Honor Society members.

Nor were all their achievements purely academic. Over half were either class- or student-body-elected officials their senior year, about a quarter worked on school publications, and nearly three-quarters of the class participated in varsity athletics in secondary school.

It is safe to say that most civilian college and university directors of admissions would have been delighted to see the Academy class of 1968 enter their institutions in September of 1964.

Important as academics and curriculum are at Annapolis today, the Naval Academy cannot be understood without an examination of its other concerns. The mission of the Academy reads, in part: "To develop midshipmen morally, mentally and physically and to imbue them with the highest ideals of duty, honor, and loyalty. . . ." These are ambitious words and they make it clear that the Academy sees its duty as transcending that of an ordinary civilian educational institution. The inculcation of ideals such as honor and loyalty is related to, but certainly goes beyond, the field of intellectual endeavor.

Speaking to the gathered parents of the entering class of 1968, the Commandant of Midshipmen, Captain Sheldon Kinney, said: "We strive constantly to imbue your son with the highest ideals of duty, honor, and loyalty. This is accomplished through precept and example and by prescribing a way of life in keeping with the requirements, customs, and traditions of the naval service. . . . You have nurtured and developed your sons; our responsibility is to continue this development in mind, body, and character. . . ." Captain Kinney was only reiterating what the Academy has taken as one of its responsibilities almost from its founding. It is this concern with character—this feeling of obligation to inculcate certain ideals—that distinguishes the Academy from most other institutions of higher learning.

How does the Academy go about this extraordinarily difficult task? Clearly, the work of the classroom, the influence and example of teachers are of great importance. But against this backdrop of education—which every college and university supplies to one degree or another—the Naval Academy applies its unique mixture of routine, discipline, and training.

In order to get at this point more effectively, let's go through part of a typical day with a midshipman.

At 6:15 in the morning every one of the 4000 or so midshipmen housed in Bancroft Hall hops out of bed at the sound of a bell that could never be mistaken for a gentle chime. One of the midshipmen in each room must immediately appear at the door to report to the watch officer that his roommates are up and doing. There is only a 30-minute interval to prepare for breakfast formation. This means shaving, dressing neatly, shining shoes, brushing uniform, and otherwise getting ready for an inspection that is held at that formation. Everyone marches to breakfast, served in a mess hall which will seat all of the midshipmen at one time. Before long, the round of classes has started.

At any time during the course of the day, the midshipman's room is susceptible to inspection—and this is no motherly check to see that pajamas are hung up. Beds must be neatly made, furniture dusted, shoes lined up properly with trees in place and laces tucked in, clothes neatly stowed, and books and papers correctly arranged. When things are not right, the midshipman in charge of the room (a privilege which is rotated among the occupants) is placed on the report and receives demerits, possible extra duty, and a corresponding drop in his conduct mark.

The idea of accountability is driven home again and again. You are responsible for the way you look, you are responsible for the condition of your room, you are responsible for correct posture, you are responsible, period. Living this way twenty-four hours a day, practically twelve months a year, inevitably leaves its mark. Call it indoctrination, call it regimentation, or call it character molding—it is the strict discipline of this daily routine, this constant accountability for four years, that is one of the Academy's main implements in achieving its aims.

For those afraid they might not be able to do it, that they might find it too demanding, I can only say that most young men do not find it so. After a time, these requirements become routine, they are accepted without thought or resentment, and, while I do not remember them as downright enjoyable, neither do I remember any feeling of frustration or undue restriction. In the long run, most men like an orderly way of living, and these habits of self-discipline and self-restraint, of neatness and of a scheduled day, remain with most Academy graduates the rest of their lives.

There are those who believe that such strict and busy routine is not compatible with intellectual endeavor, that a school which is run in such a Spartan manner must inevitably lack that thoughtful atmosphere, that air of informal tolerance which is essential to higher education. This, of course, must remain a matter of individual opinion, but my own view is that the great majority of young Americans can well use this sort of Spartan balance along with their academic endeavors. Not only is there room for both ingredients, but the very balance and contrast between the two may lead to a more productive educational experience than is the case when one of these elements is absent.

From breakfast until 3 or 4 in the afternoon, the midshipman is busy with classes, study periods, laboratory work and drills. In the early afternoon, however, begins another important ingredient in the Naval Academy system: organized athletics. Every midshipman is required to participate in some way, and there are many ways. The Academy maintains 101 acres of playing fields, it supports twenty-one different varsity squads in intercollegiate competition, and it has intramural athletic competition in everything from football to water polo.

Naval Academy teams play to win; in a typical year of competition with other colleges of the nation, Academy teams will win two-thirds of their games—and fight hard for every one. Every year sees three or four intercollegiate championship squads and a liberal sprinkling of All-Americans. In 1964, for example, the Academy had nine All-Americans in eight different sports.

Since the time of Porter and Luce, athletics have played an important role at Annapolis. They represent more than simply a means of blowing off excess energy and finding a change of pace from classroom work. Rightly or wrongly—and in my opinion, rightly—the Academy views its athletic program as an important means of fulfilling its mission to develop midshipmen "morally, mentally, and physically."

Competitive athletics require rigorous training, team effort, self-denial, and plain hard work—all for a recognized goal. While it is true that such attributes are not universally admired, they are important to a military organization dedicated to the defense of the United States. Once again, the basic aim of the Academy must be kept in mind.

Although the emphasis is on rugged, contact sports, in recent years there has been an effort to provide sports which can be carried into adult life usefully. There are fine facilities for tennis, golf, and squash, and the sailing arrangements are among the best in the country. The sailing fleet ranges from the 88-foot schooner *Freedom* down to the fleet of intercollegiate Gannett dinghies. Each Annapolis-to-Newport and Newport-to-Bermuda race sees entries from the Academy's ocean sailing fleet, and a recent gift from Cornelius Shields has made some of the beautiful 30-foot Shields class sloops available for intercollegiate racing.

Is all of this emphasis on organized athletics at the Academy justified in the world of the 1960s and 70s? The answer is not an easy one to give. If organized athletics become an end in themselves, if they take the attention and energies of the midshipmen to the exclusion of all else, then the answer must be no. Throughout my discussion of the Academy, I have attempted to emphasize the need for a proper balance between intellectual and nonintellectual endeavor, between education and training. Athletics must be kept in perspective, but they are of importance.

The aim of the Academy, mission statements aside for a moment, is to produce officers for the Navy. Officers are more than managers, engineers, and executives; they are leaders in an organization meant to fight in the defense of the nation. Naval leadership is composed of many things: intelligence, education, and imagination are highly important and increasingly so as the nation and its society mature. But there is more; the naval officer in the fleet deals with young men from many different walks of life—not all will respond to the same things. Courage, stamina, and manliness are still of great importance in the maintenance of an effective

Navy. How can such elusive qualities be cultivated? Perhaps there is no final answer, but the routine and discipline of the Academy combined with its program of highly competitive athletics constitute a formula that has not been without some success in the past.

In attempting to place the Spartan–Athenian balance at Annapolis in proper perspective, there is one other factor that must be mentioned. Few young men can spend four years in this intensive environment without obtaining a deep sense of identification with the Navy. The wearing of the uniform, the association with the officers on duty at the Academy, the constant participation in sports where one represents the Navy, the singing of Navy songs, the cheering on of other Navy teams, the summer cruises on Navy ships—all of this adds up to an important end result. By the time graduation has arrived, hearing someone else criticize the Navy is like hearing criticism of one's own family. It's all right to criticize it oneself—and all midshipmen do—but very few of them like to hear someone outside the Navy do it.

In the last analysis, this may be the most important achievement of the Academy. Claims and counterclaims about intellectual, moral, and leadership characteristics are hard to substantiate or refute. Individual examples can be shown to make almost any desired case. But statistically, one fact is irrefutable: ten years after commissioning, a higher percentage of Academy graduates remains on active duty with the Navy than of officers from any other college-level source. One hears a great deal about identity crises among college students these days. I have yet to hear of one at the Naval Academy. Everyone is reasonably sure who he is and where he is—and that he is being trained (and educated) to be an officer in the United States Navy. And, in most cases, by the time the four years are over, he feels like part of the Navy team.

In attempting to get at the essentials of the Academy during these important years of transition, we have emphasized curriculum and training. There is, most decidedly, a lighter side. On weekends there is a mass invasion of the town and yard by girls who have been invited by upperclass midshipmen (plebes rate this privilege only on one or two occasions). Nor are all the girls from far places; the town of Annapolis itself has contributed its fair share of attractive dates for midshipmen (and, eventually, wives for naval officers) over the years. Dragging, as it's called locally, has always been fun at the Academy. There are plenty of things to do: attending athletic events, afternoon tea dances, formal evening dances (called hops), sailing, tennis, and just plain walks and picnics are all possibilities.

The summers are filled with interesting experiences. After plebe year and after second-class (junior) year, they are devoted to cruises with the fleet which often includes some European ports. The summer after third-class (sophomore) year is spent in aviation indoctrination and a four-week academic program.

There are Christmas leaves of about two weeks, and two three-day breaks: one at the end of the first term in January and another in late March. Everyone takes a month-long summer leave at the end of the summer program.

No four years so filled with hard work, demanding routine, and constant accountability can be termed sheer fun. But when it is all added up, I think it can be said that the Academy represents one of the richest and most beneficial experiences open to the youth of America today.

Whatever its virtues, whatever its faults, for today's Navy the Academy produces less than 1000 officers a year—only a fraction of the 10,000 needed annually to maintain a corps of 75,000 active officers. The majority of the new officers must come from other sources. In its search for officers to meet current requirements, the Navy depends heavily on the Naval Reserve Officer Training Corps.

The idea of the citizen soldier or sailor is deeply rooted in the American heritage; from the Minutemen of Concord to the stirring call to arms after Pearl Harbor, we have cherished the image of the dropped plow and hastily seized rifle. Always distrustful of a large standing military force in peacetime, the American people have preferred a small skeleton force of professionals to be fleshed out when danger threatened.

Before the Civil War, the only civilian colleges devoted to the training of officers in peacetime were Vermont's Norwich University (founded in 1819 by a former West Point superintendent) and, more widely known, such southern military colleges as VMI and the Citadel. The contribution of these schools was, of course, small in numbers. Civilian college training for officers received its first significant boost from the Morrill Land-Grant Bill passed in 1862. This law, which made public land or money available to the states to establish colleges at which mechanical arts, agriculture, and military tactics would be taught, was the origin of the ROTC program in America.

Not much was accomplished from Civil War days until just before World War I, however. The War Department did not lay down very specific rules for the military training at the land-grant schools, and the number of officers they contributed to the Army was small, at best. The Navy did not participate in the nineteenth century land-grant military training.

In 1916, the National Defense Act incorporated a reserve officer training program that had been under consideration by the Army's General Staff for some time. Although it was too late to make a significant contribution to World War I, the ROTC program created then remained in existence after the war. The Navy was still not included, but in 1926, under legislation passed in 1925, Naval ROTC midshipmen began studies at six institutions: Harvard, Yale, Georgia Tech, Northwestern, and the Universities of Washington and California. The first class of 125 (total from the six schools) graduated in 1930, two more colleges were added in 1938, and as the country mobilized just prior to Pearl Harbor the number of colleges was increased to twenty-seven.

During World War II, the Navy switched from NROTC to a series of V-programs located at all of the existing NROTC colleges, plus a significant number of others. Early in the war, the Navy wisely commissioned about 200 men from the faculties and administrative staffs of the nation's colleges and then assigned these officers to duty in the Bureau of Naval Personnel and with individual Navy units on college campuses. These officers provided invaluable counsel as to how the nation's universities and colleges could best help produce trained officers for the national emergency.

The Navy took time during the war to study its postwar officer supply program and, as early as 1944, began to plan for an enlarged Naval ROTC to be instituted upon the return of peace. Even before the actual end of the war, the Navy terminated its emergency V-programs and returned to an NROTC organization. As early as February and March of 1945, the Bureau of Naval Personnel was indicating that the Navy hoped to have about fifty NROTC units, postwar, and was writing letters to a number of campuses sounding them out as to their willingness to be part of such a venture.

On October 30, 1945, Secretary of the Navy James Forrestal approved the report of a special board concerning NROTC, headed by Rear Admiral James Holloway, later Chief of Naval Personnel. The senior civilian member was Dr. James Phinney Baxter, then President of Williams College, and a lifelong student of naval matters.

The Holloway-Baxter board produced a report which was as remarkable for its clarity and brevity as for its vision. Mindful of the longtime Annapolis monopoly on the Navy's high positions, the board report listed as one of its aims the elimination of "sources of intra-service friction so that each officer may have a sense of equal opportunity and of belonging."

The Board recommended an expansion of the prewar ROTC program with the new feature that the Navy would pay the tuition and supporting expenses of its regular NROTC students, expecting in return a period of obligated service on the part of all NROTC graduates. It was also expected that a portion, but by no means all, of the NROTC graduates would plan to make the Navy a career. The Holloway board recognized that a Navy the size of the one then in prospect for peacetime (which, by and large, has materialized) would require a significant number of junior officers who did not intend to pursue the Navy as a lifetime career.

The Holloway Board recommended, in particular (italics added):

> a. Immediate and vigorous action to insure positive indoctrination and training of all officers in mutual understanding of the problems which must be solved in order that individual officers *from all sources may pull together for the common good of the Navy.*

b. Identical designation of all junior line officers.
c. Equal opportunity among all officers for promotion, responsibility, training, and education.
d. The adjustment of the supply of permanent commissioned officers taken into the Navy so that approximately one-half come from the Naval Academy and one-half from other sources.

The board report then went on to say:

> Implementation of the last of these measures alone will in time serve to eliminate intra-service friction and insure an open-minded, alert officer corps *wherein each source of entry provides qualities for mutual emulation.* The Marine Corps offers the Navy sound precedent. Their officers, drawn from varied sources, are unsurpassed in professional esprit.

The report of the board further provided that the regular NROTC students whose tuition was to be borne by the government would be chosen through a system of nationwide examinations and interviews similar to those used to select candidates for the V-programs during the war.

The legislation implementing the Holloway Plan, modified to provide for a supplemental number of contract NROTC students whose school expenses would not be borne by the government, was passed by the Congress in the summer of 1946 and, due at least partly to the forceful urging of Secretary James Forrestal, President Truman shortly thereafter signed the bill into law. The Navy was extremely fortunate to have obtained such legislation. The Army, for a number of reasons not germane to our subject, had not been able to request similar legislation, and there was, of course, reluctance to provide such a fine program for one service and not for the other.

The Holloway Plan has stood the test of time. Today, nearly twenty years after its inception, it operates essentially the way Admiral Holloway and Dr. Baxter intended. The Navy has taken seriously the words of the original report which spoke of equal opportunity for promotion, responsibility, training, and education. Promotion records indicate that NROTC graduates do as well as Academy graduates in selection for higher rank, and there is every reason to believe that, as time goes on and NROTC officers acquire seniority, a very sizable proportion of the Navy's flag officers will come from this program.

But what of the individual young man who decides to follow the NROTC path to a commission in the Navy? What are the requirements and how does he proceed? To begin with, his secondary school or college will have booklets giving the location and date of the annual examinations held for the Naval ROTC regular appointments. If the applicant is successful, he will be interviewed by a board of naval officers, frequently made up of men stationed nearby. If the hurdles of mental and physical examinations, interviews, and recommendations are successfully crossed, the prospective NROTC student must then be accepted by the college of his choice. During the examining process he is asked to name several of the NROTC colleges (listed in the Appendix) in order of his choice. Depending upon vacancies within the units, the Navy will try to let the successful candidate enroll in the college of his choice, but this cannot be counted upon absolutely.

When finally enrolled at one of the fifty-three colleges or universities now containing NROTC units, the NROTC midshipman will find himself with certain privileges and obligations not those of his fellow civilian students.

First of all, the Navy pays his tuition, buys his textbooks, and pays for all special equipment required by the academic departments of the college. In addition, the Navy buys all of the NROTC midshipman's uniforms and pays him a salary of $600 a year.

In return, he is required to take a course in Naval Science during all four years at the university. This usually consists of three recitations plus a drill period per week. In his freshman year, he will take a general orientation course in naval subjects such as seamanship and leadership. The sophomore course is slanted toward naval weapons and their tactical use. The junior year is devoted mainly to marine engineering and navigation, and the senior year stresses naval operations, tactics, formations, and so on.

There are two summer cruises: one between the sophomore and junior years and one between the junior and senior years. These are made in regular units of the fleet and often include visits to foreign ports. Fundamentally, they provide an opportunity to apply the principles learned during the Naval Science courses taken in the winter.

The NROTC midshipman is free, within certain limits, to take what other academic courses he will. His three hours of Naval Science constitute perhaps a fifth of his total academic work, and it is not unusual to find regular NROTC students majoring in such widely varied subjects as English literature, psychology, and mechanical engineering. Courses clearly leading to other professions, such as prelaw, premedical, predental and theological courses are, quite reasonably, not permitted.

The NROTC midshipman is normally required to wear his uniform only at weekly drill or laboratory and special naval occasions. During the summer cruise, of course, the uniform is worn at all times, and the NROTC midshipmen are subject to the same naval administration and discipline as other naval personnel.

Upon graduation, the regular NROTC midshipman is commissioned as an ensign in the Navy. He may, at the end of four years, apply for release from active duty and commissioning in the inactive Naval Reserve.

The contract NROTC midshipmen follow much the same course, except that the government does not pay their tuition, they make only one, not two, summer cruises, and upon graduation they are commissioned in the Naval Reserve instead of the regular Navy. Their period of obligated service is three years. Contract midshipmen do, however, have their Naval Science textbooks supplied by the government, their uniforms are furnished, and in their last two years, they receive a ration allowance of about $30 per month.

The Naval ROTC program is injecting a sizable number of career officers into the Navy with a college experience significantly different from that obtained at the Naval Academy. What has been the result?

Thus far, the report can only be a favorable one. The new outlooks and broader viewpoints which have entered the Navy's officer corps from the nation's campuses have strengthened and invigorated the corps. Many a wardroom where Academy officers and others work together has found that the Holloway Report of 1945 spoke the truth when it said that each source of officers might provide "qualities for mutual emulation." This has been a two-way street; each group has been able to contribute something to the other.

I can speak from personal experience of the NROTC officers who have served with me in my ships. Although many do not have academic backgrounds slanted towards technical areas, they have all shown themselves adaptable to the demanding engineering duties in submarines. My chief engineer officer in the *Skate*, for example, had been an English literature major at Northwestern. No officer who has ever served with me has been more competent or knowledgeable concerning nuclear power. Obviously, he applied himself long and hard at the Navy's nuclear-power schools; some extra effort was required, but the important point is that he not only did it, he did it extremely well and in the midst of some pretty tough competition.

Our wardroom was a richer and better place because of these officers. The give-and-take, the sense of mutual help, and the willingness to recognize other attitudes and other points of view were all beneficial to the ship as a whole. A Navy with officers from a variety of sources inevitably has advantages over one where there is absolute uniformity of background. The entire nation can point with pride to the Naval ROTC program. It is helping to harness the enormous power and capability of our universities—one of America's most important assets—to the construction of a better Navy.

Altogether, the Naval Academy, the regular NROTC, and the contract NROTC contribute about 3000 officers per year to the Navy. This number totals less than a third of the new officers required annually. To supply the rest, the Navy turns to a number of programs, none as ambitious or as career-oriented as the Academy or the NROTC, but all nevertheless vital to the support of the Navy.

The largest program numerically is the Officer Candidate School at Newport, Rhode Island. This is a highly concentrated sixteen-week course in naval science conducted for officer candidates for the line, restricted line, special duty only, and staff corps. To be eligible, one must be between nineteen and twenty-seven (except for lawyers, who may be thirty-three) and possess a baccalaureate degree from an accredited college. Physical qualifications vary depending upon the type of commission being sought. Graduates of the Officer Candidate School are commissioned in the Naval Reserve and have a two-year period of obligated service.

Closely related to the OCS program is the Reserve Officer Candidate (ROC) program in which selected college students who are members of the Naval Reserve attend eight-week courses for two summers at the OCS establishment in Newport. Upon graduation from college, ROC members who have successfully completed the two summer courses are commissioned ensigns in the Naval Reserve line, Supply Corps, and Civil Engineer Corps.

The Navy has not forgotten the Waves in its postwar officer programs. Qualified college women, both juniors and seniors, may join the WAVE OCS program and, after taking eight weeks of training at the Women's OCS in Newport, earn an ensign's commission. After they are commissioned ensigns, they take eight more weeks of training before they are assigned to active duty. The college juniors may take the first eight-week course during the summer vacation preceding their senior year. All WAVE officer commissions at present are in the Naval Reserve.

The remaining officer programs can be categorized under three broad headings: aviation, medical, and programs designed to make it possible for qualified enlisted men of the Navy to attain officer status.

There are three aviation programs and each of them is designed to produce both pilots and other aviation officers. The first of the aviation programs is closely related to the ROC concept; selected college students spend two of their summer vacations taking eight-week courses, but instead of being at Newport they are conducted at the pre-flight school at Pensacola. Upon graduation from college, the AVROC program members are commissioned as ensigns in the Naval Reserve. Those who volunteer and are qualified then commence their eighteen months of flight training as ensigns; AVROC ensigns who plan to become Naval Aviation Officers, Ground Support Officers, or other non-flying members of the naval aviation structure, take further training at the Pensacola Naval Aviation Officer School before being assigned to operation units.

The second aviation program is designated Aviation Officer Candidate (AOC) and is open to men between nineteen and twenty-six who have a baccalaureate degree in an acceptable field from an accredited college. Candidates may be married. The AOCS take the sixteen-week Pre-Flight course described in Chapter 3, and upon completion are commissioned ensigns in the Naval Reserve, and complete their flight training in that category. AOC ensigns who do not wish to become pilots attend the Naval Aviation Officer School.

The last aviation program, the Naval Aviation Cadet program, accepts men who have completed only two years of college. Enlisted men who can satisfactorily pass qualifying examinations may be admitted with a waiver on the formal education requirement. The NavCads who will fly take the full eighteen-month course before they are commissioned ensigns in the Naval Reserve. Non-flying NavCads (more accurately known as Officer Candidate Airmen, or OCANS), take an approximately thirteen-month course before they are commissioned and sent to duty as aviation officers or ground support officers within operational units.

The OCS, ROC, and aviation programs together supply some 5000 new officers to the Navy annually, and thus constitute the major source of new officers. However, most of these officers are in the Naval Reserve and do not plan to make the Navy a career. Such a large turnover has many disadvantages, but it has the very tangible advantage of producing a steady supply of reserve officers on inactive duty who have a valuable background of training and experience. The mobilization potential of such a group is hard to express in quantitative terms, but it represents a significant factor in the overall military potential of the United States.

There is a variety of programs for commissioning officers in the medical, dental, and nursing fields. In addition to those for the direct appointment, as lieutenants, of newly graduated doctors and dentists (interested medical and dental students should consult their schools for the details of these arrangements), there are programs for naval enlisted personnel to receive training and, ultimately, commissions in the Medical Service Corps. These men (and women) work in such fields as optometry, podiatry, pharmacy, and hospital administration.

Junior and senior women students in accredited schools of nursing may become members of the Navy Nurse Corps Candidate Program, have their tuition and all educational expenses paid, receive a small retainer salary, and become commissioned ensigns in the Naval Reserve six months prior to graduation, at which time they begin to receive an ensign's full pay. Upon completion of their nurse training they are assigned within the Navy's medical organization. Under the Nursing Education program, enlisted women in the Navy may enter civilian nursing schools under a similar government-tuition-support concept and win a commission in the Nurse Corps.

The last broad category of officer programs is that intended primarily for the enlisted men of the fleet. The largest numerically is the limited-duty-officer (LDO) path to a commission. At one time this was primarily a means for direct appointment of experienced and qualified petty officers to the rank of ensign. Recently the concept has been changed to provide primarily for the appointment of these men as warrant officers.

Supplementing the LDO program is a concept whereunder junior enlisted or warrant personnel (both men and women) who have completed thirty semester hours at an accredited college or have high school degrees and can pass certain qualifying examinations may be appointed as officers in the unrestricted line or staff corps.

Lastly, the Navy Enlisted Scientific Program (NESEP) provides qualified enlisted men of the fleet an uninterrupted four-year college education leading to a degree in engineering, science, or mathematics. The NESEP men take their college course in enlisted status, receive full government support while doing so, and may be married upon entering the program. Upon receiving their college degrees, they report to the Officer Candidate School in Newport (or Pre-Flight in Pensacola if they want to become aviation officers), where they undergo the normal programs before commissioning. At present more than twenty colleges and universities are taking part in the NESEP program, including M.I.T., Purdue, Stanford, and Vanderbilt.

All told, there are fifteen separate programs leading to a commission in the Navy aside from the Naval Academy and the NROTC. The majority of the new officers entering the Navy each year come from these programs, where the total naval indoctrination and training period averages about sixteen weeks of work ashore. What is the result?

The answer is perhaps best given by relating an experience I had during my first summer cruise as a Naval Academy midshipman.

The summer cruises were, and remain, a most important part of the Naval Academy and NROTC concept. Here is a chance to see the Navy at first hand, to work under conditions which approximate those experienced by the enlisted men of the fleet, to learn things about the Navy which cannot be obtained from a book. The chance to get to know some of the Navy's enlisted men, working in their regular environment, is one of the most valuable byproducts of the cruise. Inevitably some information that is not strictly official (and not likely to be sanctioned by either parents or naval authorities) gets exchanged during these associations, but by and large the process is a wholesome and profitable one for all concerned.

I remember particularly the first-class boatswain's mate who was in charge of the deck work in our division in the old battleship *New York*. He had been in the ship for years, and it seemed to our youthful perspective that he had been in the Navy forever. He was a strict taskmaster and apparently had little liking for midshipmen. In any event, he made our lives miserable on many occasions, and it was only toward the last of the three-months cruise that I even had an opportunity to talk with him.

It would be exaggerating to say that he unbent, but he did loosen up to the extent of confessing that he knew he gave the midshipmen a hard time but he did it because he thought it his duty. "I never had any real home before the Navy and it's all I have now—what I do for the Navy, I'll try to do right," he added.

He then shifted from a sort of half-official, half-comradely tone of voice and said, "I kin take officers or leave 'em alone. But if we're gonna have 'em, they ought to be good ones." Something in the way he said this made me realize that in his way he was trying to say a good bit more. I replied that I agreed but there wasn't much I could do now except try to do a good job at the Academy.

"That Academy," grunted the sailor. "One thing I gotta admit —I wouldn't go through that four years of (unprintable) for all the gold braid in the Navy. They earn what they git and, as far as I'm concerned, they kin have it." The boatswain's mate spat expertly into a container about ten feet off and walked away.

The Navy has changed in the quarter of a century since that conversation took place. First of all, the boatswain's mate wouldn't talk that way today, in all likelihood. He would be a better-educated man, and he would also be aware that most officers in today's Navy do not get their commissions by "going through" anything, but rather by virtue of the fact that they are college graduates. The proving ground for officers today usually comes after commissioning rather than before.

Before World War II, an ensign of the line had been relatively thoroughly trained and indoctrinated prior to putting on his uniform. The odds were heavy that he was an Academy graduate and that he had little thought of anything but making the Navy his career. Today's new ensign, in the majority of cases, reports to his ship with only his sixteen weeks of indoctrination. His main asset is his education, and this may not be directly applicable to the problems at hand in any but the most general way.

These young men are thrown very much more on their own resources of ingenuity, hard work, and knowledge of human relations in general for success in their assignments. Some are highly adaptable and soon are pulling their weight in the ship; others seem ill-suited for the life from the beginning and, had they been subjected to a longer period of training, might well have fallen by the wayside. There is a greater load on the commanding officers; in a way, it is a return to the ancient system of training officers on board ship. The necessities of the modern world have brought us full cycle to the systems of another day.

One of the many factors which has made the post-commission training of officers increasingly successful has been the growth of what many call our "Naval University"—the variety of fleet training schools, factory-based schools, aviation and submarine training complexes, type schools for amphibious and destroyer officers, and the various short refresher courses available in almost every major base. While the submarine and aviation training courses are usually of longer duration, the others, and particularly the refresher training courses, are short enough so that officers can be detached from ships temporarily to take advantage of them. Thus, practical training in subjects such as navigation, shipboard engineering, ship handling, electronics, communications, sonar, naval law, damage control, and even leadership may be obtained. This growing complex of *ad hoc* schools has decreased the need for strictly practical training before commissioning, and fits in well with the increased emphasis on academic work at the Academy as well as with the fact that the majority of the Navy's new officers each year have had little or no practical shipboard experience prior to commissioning.

Important as this increased trend toward post-commission training is, however, it is overshadowed by the Navy's plans for the post-commission education of its officers. These can be divided into two broad categories: academic postgraduate education at the Navy's own school at Monterey (as well as at civilian universities), and military courses at the Naval War College and the nation's three joint military colleges.

Formal postgraduate education, particularly in technical subjects, has a long history in the Navy, going back to 1912, when the Naval Postgraduate School was formally established on the grounds of the Academy at Annapolis. In those days the curriculum called for one year of study at Annapolis followed by two more at such schools as M.I.T., Columbia, Harvard, Chicago, and Michigan, depending upon the technical specialty being pursued.

In December of 1951, the postgraduate school was moved from Annapolis to Monterey, and it now offers a wide variety of graduate courses. Taking cognizance of the increasing need for officers with education and experience in the field of international relations, the Navy offers postgraduate courses in this field at Harvard, American University, Tufts, and the University of California. The engineering officers of the restricted line continue their rigorous three-year course at M.I.T. which has been the foundation of their professional education for many years.

Postgraduate academic education is now usually undertaken by officers during the middle phase of their careers (seven to twelve years of service), and, of course, is normally restricted to career officers.

In the military field, the Naval War College at Newport offers both a junior (command and staff) course for officers at the lieutenant-commander level and a senior course for commanders and captains. Of increasing interest and importance to all of the services are the three joint service colleges: the Armed Forces Staff College at Norfolk, the Industrial College of the Armed Forces at Washington, and the National War College, also at Washington.

The Naval War College and the joint service colleges all contribute significantly to the professional education and outlook of the Navy's career officers. By the time an officer is eligible for the first of these schools (Naval War College command and staff course or the Armed Forces Staff College) he usually has had twelve or more years of commissioned service. Only officers who are sure about making the Navy their career attend, and each officer has to some degree made a reputation for himself through his operational experiences. Although there will be ships to command and airplanes to fly in the future, the career officer's attention begins to center itself more on assignments concerned with planning, logistics, international relations, and other such matters that will prepare him for higher command.

The War College's command and staff course and the Armed Forces Staff College both emphasize such matters as planning large operations; the writing of operation orders, plans, and concepts; the conduct of feasibility checks for logistic arrangements; and command relationships in multi-service operations. The Armed Forces Staff College has particular responsibility for courses in the planning of joint operations in which all of the services participate.

The Industrial College of the Armed Forces and the National War College, both located on the attractive grounds of Fort Leslie J. McNair at the confluence of the Potomac and the Anacostia Rivers, are attended mainly by officers with about twenty years service. Both prepare officers for assignments in policy-making on the Pentagon staffs.

These military colleges form an important part of the middle grade and senior officer's education in the Navy. Not only is the actual content of the school curriculum of great importance, but the association with officers of other services and civilian branches of the government yields very significant dividends. Almost a quarter of the National War College student body is made up of civilian personnel from the State Department, United States Information Agency, Central Intelligence Agency, Department of Commerce, Bureau of Budget, Department of Defense, and National Security Agency. There is both give and take; not only do the officers learn to understand and respect the civilian role in the government's policy-making partnership, but civilian students at the colleges also come away with a more balanced understanding of the role of military power in national policy.

In closing our discussion of the education of today's naval officers, it might be well to step back and make a quick review for perspective.

The Navy maintains an officer corps of some 75,000 men and women, of whom roughly 10,000 must be replaced each year due to losses from retirement, resignation, and release from active duty. Of these new officers, the Navy attempts to provide a four-year period of education and training for only a portion; the Naval Academy and NROTC contribute about 3000 per year, and it is from this group, in the main, that career line officers are chosen.

For the rest, the Navy depends mainly upon the civilian colleges and universities of the nation to provide doctors, dentists, chaplains, supply officers, civil engineers, and the remaining line officers. The staff officers are usually commissioned by direct appointment after completion of the necessary education; the non-Academy and non-NROTC line officers are supplied by a variety of programs, most of them designed to take young men or women with college education, provide them with a short period of naval indoctrination, and commission them in the Naval Reserve.

Although the majority of the reserve officers who are commissioned through these programs leave the Navy after two or three years, there is an opportunity for them to apply for transfer to the regular Navy and become career officers. A sizable number of young officers, of both the line and staff, transfer to the regular Navy in this manner each year, and experience is showing that they are able to compete with their Academy and NROTC contemporaries very successfully indeed.

In perspective, the system is complex and varied, but the size and nature of the Navy today demand such an approach. Details will doubtless change, but so long as the United States maintains a Navy of its present size, an officer-education system which meshes a variety of means for educating career, reserve, staff, and other types of officers will be necessary. Further, the system of providing continuing education at academic postgraduate schools as well as at senior defense colleges will grow in importance.

The Navy is shaped by the society it exists to defend; as that society evolves ever more swiftly, it depends more and more upon education to solve its problems. So, inevitably, does the Navy.

CHAPTER FIVE

What about Naval Officers' Families?

A few years ago the Navy announced that henceforth the forms used by commanding officers to report on the fitness and aptitude of the officers serving under them would contain a space in which suitable comment could be made on the officer's wife—on her ability to assist her husband in his chosen career, and particularly upon her ability to represent the United States in duty assignments abroad.

Perhaps not surprisingly, there were many editorials in the public press against the move. Most of them argued that a man's wife was his own affair and that judgment on her suitability in an officer's official record was improper at the least, if not downright un-American.

Without question, some very important factors in our lives are best left undiscussed—and particularly in official records. The newspapers were right in this respect. And yet, the officers who had proposed the change in the reporting forms were acting on a legitimate concern—a naval officer's wife is of great importance to his career, as well as to the Navy, and indeed, in some instances, to the United States itself. While it is true that the wife of any professional person—minister, doctor, lawyer, or teacher—may prove of great advantage or detriment to her husband's career, the burden and responsibility of a naval officer's wife is an extraordinarily heavy one.

Let us see if we can take an objective look at what a naval officer's wife can expect in the Navy of the 1960s and 1970s, what her children can expect, and what the family life of a naval officer is.

There are, of course, all sorts of stereotyped ideas about naval officers' wives and families. Most of them are wrong or, at best, apply to a Navy that is long gone. Public quarters, automobiles furnished by the Navy, servants furnished by the Navy, gala social whirls, and free travel throughout the world may or may not be part of your mental image of family life in the Navy; but in any event, such a gay picture has no relation to present reality.

The Navy family of today typically lives in a rented home in a part of the community that is predominantly civilian. More and more frequently, though, the home is self-owned; the economy seems to be increasingly geared to permit the successful purchase and sale of a home over a two- or three-year period and, indeed, many a young Navy family has started its first financial gain this way. But rented or owned, the home is almost always the problem and responsibility of the Navy family; public quarters in the Navy are rare, and it is probably correct to say that the typical Navy family occupies them only once or twice in the course of a career.

There are at least as many advantages as disadvantages to such an arrangement. A naval officer's pay consists in part of an allowance for quarters; if public quarters are occupied, this amount is deducted. While it is usually a lesser amount than the cost of maintaining a comparable home in the civilian community, the opportunities for building a financial equity as well as sheer pride of ownership in one's own home should not be overlooked. In addition, there are many rewards to being part of the civilian community. A balance is created between one's service friends and those of the civilian community. One often develops an informed view of community problems, and the community itself is apt to be more understanding and sympathetic in its attitude toward a government establishment whose representatives live and take part in the community as a whole. In short, it's good public relations.

Leaving the subject of quarters, Navy families furnish their own transportation. The use of official Navy vehicles is closely controlled, and the wise naval officer solves his own transportation problems for all affairs except those of a strictly official nature—and the interpretation of what is official must be narrow. Needless to say, it almost never includes families.

Except in the case of a few senior officers, occupying public quarters, whose official duties include a great deal of entertaining, the Navy supplies no servants for the homes of its officers. This is as it should be, and young Navy families contemplating the decades ahead will be well advised not to make "the day when we have stewards in the house" part of their plans.

Now, having put public quarters, official cars, and servants out of the picture, let's look at some of the more positive aspects of Navy family life.

First and foremost, no naval officer and no Navy wife can look at the Navy as just another job. Not even to the extent that the wife of a doctor, dentist, or lawyer can detach herself from her husband's work can the Navy wife live a life separate from the Navy. Navy customs are changing from those which dominated the first half of this century, but the new ones are nearly as pervasive as the old, and slowly but surely the Navy way of life makes its influence felt.

Here again, some public misconceptions need to be set aside: although it is true that the Navy makes certain social activities close to an obligation, the image of Navy families leading a gay life of cocktail parties, dinners, and receptions is simply erroneous. The great majority of Navy families lack the money, servants, or inclination to follow such a course; most of them engage in such activities to no greater extent than their civilian contemporaries in comparable income groups.

There are, however, some social obligations in the Navy which do not exist in civilian life. There remains a tradition of graciousness and hospitality that, although it is a remnant of days gone by, adds much to the pleasure of life in the Navy. Except in Washington, calls are traditionally made upon one's commanding officer soon after reporting to a new station and, in many cases, just before detachment. These calls are not announced, are traditionally made in the afternoon on weekends, are always short (fifteen or twenty minutes); and cards are left whether or not those visited were actually at home. The call is considered complete in either event. The calls are returned according to the same set of customs.

Such calls, while perhaps unfamiliar to a generation reared in the informality of today, have many dividends not immediately apparent. They more or less insure that Navy families will be organized and presentable for formal callers on weekend afternoons—not a bad custom whatever the reason. Moreover, they bring young officers into the homes of their seniors early in a tour of duty, and provide an opportunity for a relationship to develop which is warmer than that provided in official circles. Finally, many an observant young Navy wife has taken advantage of such calls to note those customs of decor, taste, and conversation which make up one of the intangible legacies passed on from Navy family to Navy family.

Calls of this sort are an important part of the Navy social custom, and the young officer who nails down his senior with a phone call before making the effort to get dressed, who asks for an evening call, or who fails to leave cards when his senior is not at home, is displaying his lack of respect for one of the delicate differences between the Navy and just another job. It may be true that every one of such actions can be defended in the name of "common sense," but the fact remains that some of the most precious aspects of the Navy heritage do not quite jibe with "common sense"—perhaps therein lies their uncommon value.

When Navy families entertain for dinner, there are similar unwritten customs that originated in a more gracious day, when servants were a reality, not a memory. Nevertheless, these customs persist today and their prospects for continued life are good. Cocktails are almost invariably served; drinking in moderation is a part of Navy social life. However, the word moderate is important—the naval officer or his wife who even once or twice has too much to drink is violating a naval custom of just as much importance as any other one I know.

When there are guests, dinners are usually served by candlelight, and more often than not, a dry table wine is provided. Coffee is served in the living room after dinner from a silver service as gracious as the host can reasonably afford. Brandy and liqueurs usually, but not always, follow. The old custom of separating the men from the ladies for coffee and brandy is dying out in the Navy as it did long ago in civilian life. However, in a few families it is still encountered; in such situations, needless to say, the Navy wife who barges into the midst of the gentlemen prematurely because she is "tired of talking to all those girls" is not showing the proper respect for the wishes of her hostess.

One remains at least an hour after the coffee is served and is, if at all possible, careful not to leave before one's seniors. This custom places an obligation on the seniors to leave a dinner party reasonably promptly, and most of them do. The obligation, of course, does not stop there. Nothing is so depressing to a tired hostess—who has doubtless spent the day preparing the meal—as a young dinner guest who goes on tirelessly into the night firmly convinced that his sparkling conversation is holding everyone spellbound. Nothing is so priceless as the knack of knowing when to go home. Those who rise to go and then spend the next half hour standing in the doorway continuing to exude charm and gaiety are as unwelcome in the Navy as elsewhere.

Aside from calls and dinner parties, there is one other aspect of organized Navy social life worthy of special note: that concerning the activities undertaken by the wives alone. It is only to be expected that, in a calling in which husbands are often gone for long periods of time, the wives have formed the custom over the years of socializing both formally and informally.

Ladies' teas are dying a slow but probably well-deserved death in the Navy; from all that I have heard of them, they are one of the sound reasons for appreciating one's manhood. However, the ladies' luncheon survives in hardy form—often with a beleaguered male speaker bravely appearing after the cold asparagus. Although Navy wives vary in their enthusiasm for such activities, they have their importance and are part of the Navy wife's responsibility, whatever her views. In this connection, the wishes of the commanding officer's wife are important. Within the bounds of reason, she can and often does call the tune on activities of this nature. This fact, obviously, places responsibility on the wives of senior officers to be considerate, reasonable, and helpful in the conduct of such customs. By far the great majority are just that; an occasional encounter with one who is not will merely test the mettle of the young Navy wife. Inherent taste, kindness, and good judgment are as important in the Navy as out.

Navy wives help each other. They form one of the most remarkable real estate intelligence networks in America, and their ability to size up teachers, schools, dentists, good service stations (who will genuinely help when husbands are away), and other functional aspects of a Navy town are deservedly famous. In short, much more than idle gossip is exchanged at Navy wives' get-togethers, and those who cut themselves off from them are missing part of the fun and usefulness of Navy life.

Aside from formal social activities (which I have not pretended to cover exhaustively), there are many informal social customs of importance in the Navy.

One of the first and foremost is that a Navy wife does not get into her husband's business. The old Navy was replete with stories of admirals' wives who insisted on certain niceties in, say, the uniforms of enlisted men in their husbands' commands; but this sort of thing, if it ever existed, is gone. Although no one admires the Navy wife who gushingly insists that she does not know the difference between a submarine and a destroyer, the salty wife who uses Navy slang and freely dispenses her latest opinions on selection boards, orders to officers, and Navy personalities is even less appreciated.

Similarly, the wise and tasteful Navy wife will avoid having her house or apartment look like a branch of the Naval History Museum. Mementoes and photographs of her husband's career are better restricted to den and recreation room than displayed all over the living room. Although this may be a personal prejudice, I believe the large and garish oil of father done up in uniform complete with trimmings ("by a remarkably talented young fellow we met by chance in Naples") may also be omitted from the well-tempered Navy living room.

Ostentation is as unwelcome in the Navy as elsewhere, and if private good fortune, hard work, or intelligent planning has enabled you to have an income beyond that provided by the Navy, you will be well advised not to make it overwhelmingly apparent in the way you live. Everyone knows your Navy salary to the penny, and one of the blessings in Navy life is freedom from any attempt to create an impression of affluence—whether it exists or not.

If the Navy ideal of social life can be reduced to a single phrase, it is quiet good taste and graciousness on a limited income. There is an understandable resentment of those who violate this well-established ethic.

I cannot, in this short chapter, pretend to cover all the aspects of Navy social life, and for those who want to read further in this area I recommend Florence Ridgely Johnson's well-known book, *Welcome Aboard.* For several years now, this book has served as a reliable and appreciated guide for Navy wives. Long may it thrive. However, since Mrs. Johnson had no children of her own, she very sensibly has little to say on one important aspect of married life in the Navy—the children.

A book could—and some day should—be written on this subject. The Navy wife bears a difficult responsibility toward her husband and his career. She must be many things to him—and to his associates. She must be above reproach in her personal conduct and appearance and yet tolerant of the shortcomings of others; she must be ready to make intellectual conversation with those who like such things and ready to talk trivia with those who prefer lighter chatting; she must entertain graciously without servants; she must be knowledgeable about the Navy and yet refrain from sounding that way; she must be ready to move across the country, often with little or no warning, and establish a new home in a few days. And yet all of these challenges are as nothing compared with that of providing a sound home environment for her children as they grow.

Children, fundamentally, like to stay put. When they are small, they do not understand the many uprootings of their home and the shift to new surroundings. It takes firm understanding, love, and effort on the part of Navy parents to provide the sense of security which is so important to young children, in spite of sudden moves to different parts of the world. When they are older, it is perhaps even more difficult. High school children form friendships and fall into situations in school that are difficult to uproot. What to do about the boy who has been elected president of his junior class in high school and then has to move? What about the girl who has finally found a French teacher able to straighten out the hitherto unsolvable? What about the boy on the varsity wrestling team who is moving to a school where there is no wrestling team? These problems may seem trivial in the abstract; believe me, they are not in real life.

Then, there is the problem of father's long absences. Sometimes a boy of ten or twelve runs into problems that are terribly difficult for a mother to solve alone; at the very least the task of solving children's problems alone from time to time creates one of the Navy wife's severest tests.

There are, on the other hand, tremendous advantages for Navy children, and they do, in the long run, seem to more than balance the disadvantages if the parents are willing and able to provide the necessary ingredients. Navy children become used to change; they make new friends relatively easily; they have a special feeling of warmth and attachment to their families that is not always duplicated elsewhere; and, despite their many moves from school to school, they seem to do as well as or better than their contemporaries in obtaining admittance to competitive colleges these days.

Adversity creates its own compensations, and most Navy families take their responsibilities toward their children very seriously. In many a Navy town the central leadership of the Sunday school programs, the scouting programs, and the PTA comes from Navy families. Whatever the shortcomings of these particular institutions, the participation of Navy families reflects a determination to provide the best possible activities for their children.

As usual, however, the real solution lies at home, and most Navy families are very conscious of this. Books, records, good prints, and a wholesome atmosphere are the rule in most Navy homes. Although I do not know actual statistics, I am reasonably certain that the percentage of Navy families attending church is above the national average in professional homes, and that the divorce rate is similarly below the national average.

Frequent moves combined with occasional long absences of the head of the family when his ship is away have a strong tendency to bind families closely together, and there is, within the majority of Navy families, a very heartwarming loyalty and family spirit exceeding that usually found in more settled families.

In the last analysis, however, the Navy is not the determining factor in the rearing of children in Navy families. The parents, and above all the mother, must have the background and determination to create a sound environment for the children. If that environment is there, even frequent moves from coast to coast cannot unsettle the basic source from which the children derive their ideals.

Not all Navy families succeed with their children—nor do all their civilian counterparts. But no young man contemplating the Navy as a career should allow doubts as to his ability to provide a successful home for his children to deter him. Let him, if he can, ask himself if he and his prospective (real or imagined) wife are up to the task of rearing their children successfully. For it will depend upon them to a far greater extent than upon the Navy—or any other career.

"Security" is a vastly overrated word. Young men who are worthy of their salt will not enter the naval career in its pursuit. If they do, they will be disappointed in the long run, for there are as many obstacles in the course of the successful Navy career as in any other.

However, for the Navy wife, there are certain genuine security considerations that she should not overlook. Although the details vary as from time to time Congress changes legislation, the fundamental fact is that the widow of a naval officer who dies on active duty realizes very substantial benefits not open to her civilian counterparts.

In addition, her husband's pay is secure and not subject to interruptions because of illness or injury. Similarly, the Navy family is protected from bills for medical expenses. Navy medical care is genuinely good and, within my nearly twenty-six years of association with the Navy, has noticeably improved. Many years can go by during which this benefit means no more than protection from trifling bills for children's sniffles. Then suddenly, as it did in my family not long ago, a serious and expensive illness can strike that could, quite literally, wipe out a lifetime of savings.

In these cases, the Navy has expert professional talent, the finest in facilities, and a depth of personal care and warmth of interest that could not be purchased at any price. The young officer must remember that as he goes along in the Navy he will make friends in the medical service as well as in other parts of the Navy; these men can be friends in the time of need in a sense that cannot be understood by those who have not experienced the sudden and grave illness of a family member.

I have heard complaints about Navy medical attention for more than a quarter of a century; I have yet to experience one genuine instance of incompetence or indifference in the face of real need. Short tempers in the face of imagined ills or demands for special services are another matter; it's difficult to see how such reactions can be eliminated in a system where highly trained medical men work long hours for fixed (and comparatively modest) salaries.

No one of much potential value enters a field of work with his eye fixed firmly upon its retirement benefits. Nevertheless, the prospective Navy wife, particularly, might contemplate for a moment the fact that the Navy provides a very attractive retirement program for its career officers. At the end of thirty years of service, a reasonably successful naval officer can look forward to a retirement income for life which will provide a comfortable, if not affluent, existence. Most Navy families have a good opportunity to observe possible retirement areas at first hand, and most make a sensible and comfortable choice.

Perhaps a word of caution on the subject of retirement is in order. We have been discussing customs, and I think it is appropriate to point out that the officer (of any grade) who quite obviously has his eye on retirement, knows all about its details, and talks frequently about the various injustices being perpetrated by the Congress, the Navy Department, or others, upon the great ranks of the retired is making a professional error. The purpose and spirit of the Navy do not have room for the officer who is devoting most of his attention to feathering his own retirement nest. Although nothing obviously may be done about him, the wheels of Navy justice seem to have a way of working in these cases.

If death comes to the retired officer before it does to his wife, government pension allowances may make a significant addition to whatever private insurance benefits she may expect. In short, although the Congressman who complained that the government takes lavish care of its naval officers "from the day they enter Annapolis until they enter the grave" was perhaps exaggerating, it is true that the naval officer who conducts his personal financial affairs with a reasonable care has little reason to worry about security, medical care, or comfortable life after retirement—either for himself or for his family.

First and last, however, the naval officer's life is one of service. His professional responsibility depends upon his loyalty to his nation, to the Navy, to his ship, to his men, and to his superior officers. Courage and honor are important ingredients of his personal ethics and, by the very definition of his profession, he foregoes the opportunity for large personal gain, for affluent circumstances, and for security. His wife must, to a very large degree, share these aspirations and voluntary renunciations.

If she does not understand the deep meaning of these terms, if she will receive no sense of reward from them, if loyalty, courage, and honor seem like words from another century to her, then rough seas will lie ahead. If every question must be decided on purely rational terms, if the idea of deference and respect to one's seniors—simply because they are one's seniors—seems intellectually unacceptable, then careful thought should be taken.

But most wives—and most people—are not like that. The ideas of loyalty, friendship, and honor appeal to most of us; we like the concept of dedicating ourselves to the ideals of a service that has long enjoyed an honored and very special place within our national scene. I have tried hard to be objective, to point out those things in married life within the Navy that can cause trouble, but in the main, I can do nothing except recommend it heartily.

I would like to end with a brief tribute to the Navy wives of today. Faced with more strenuous operating schedules and, in general, a more difficult task than that of a generation ago, their performance in the majority of cases is superb. The wives of commanding officers help out to a very significant degree with the wives of junior officers and enlisted men who have troubles when the ship is away. Similarly, the wives of the junior officers are often of real help in problems of their contemporaries and subordinates.

By far the great majority provide the solid, dependable kind of home management that husbands must have if they are to do their own jobs adequately when away from home. No man can do his work properly when he is wondering whether or not his children are being cared for, whether or not home finances are in order, or—perhaps most important of all—whether he has a faithful wife at home. Both as junior officer and as commanding officer I have seen some heartrending examples of how wrong things can get when the wrong sort of person takes on the responsibilities of being a Navy wife. Let me only say again that the vast majority of wives deserve nothing but praise in this regard.

Lastly, we have all noticed so many times that some families seem to like it everywhere. There are no "bad places to have duty" to them; they seem to find interesting and rewarding activities wherever they go, while other families are just the reverse. Everything is wrong all of the time.

The answer, I believe, lies most of the time with the wives and mothers of these families. A positive and cheerful attitude, and a willingness to overlook difficulties are great assets in every walk of life. For Navy wives, they are close to necessities. But for those fortunate ladies who can turn the trick, who can fulfill the responsibilities of keeping a Navy husband and family happy, I know of no fuller, happier, more varied life.

CHAPTER SIX

Is It Really a Profession?

It is late at night and the half-dark corridors of the hospital are deserted. Their black-and-white checkered floors recede in both directions without interruption except for the occasional red glow of an exit light. Overhead, a framed glass panel soundlessly flashes the call numbers of doctors wanted somewhere within the hospital. The same numbers appear again and again, always in the same sequence, apparently always without success.

An open door on the corridor leads into a waiting room in which a young man, in shirtsleeves and with tousled hair, smokes a cigarette and paces restlessly back and forth. The room has a depressing, institutional look with its garish fluorescent light; one of the tubes is faulty, but the constant hum and occasional blink go unnoticed by the young man, who adds another cigarette to the already-full ashtray.

He moves to the door and once more studies the electric call sign with its incessantly repeating sequence of numbers. He wonders if the doctors are really needed and, if so, why someone doesn't go and get them. Do the doctors ever look at the sign? Are they even in the hospital? Are they being called for his wife?

Moving away from the door, the young man looks at his watch and realizes that hours have gone by since he should have heard from the delivery room. What is going on? Is his wife safe? And what of the baby, their first child?

What is it that permits a scene similar to this to be enacted many times each night across our land and almost always achieve a happy ending? Why does our young man entrust all that he holds dearest in the world to the skill and knowledge of a stranger whose competence he has no way to judge? What is the source of such faith in another man?

The answer lies in a single term: professional standards. Our society insists on certain standards of training and professional competence before it permits a man to present himself to the public as a doctor of medicine. These standards are nation-wide; they enable an expectant father to spend his cheerless night of waiting with the knowledge that professional standards exist which go far toward ensuring that his wife and new child are in competent hands.

He cannot, of course, be certain. Tragedies do occur, doctors do make mistakes, and some cases are beyond human help—but the heavy probability is on the side of competence. The professional pride and standards of the medical profession are important and tangible assets in our society.

The doctor of medicine remains the primary and best example of the professional man in the United States today. His qualifications for that title and the rewards deriving from it go relatively unchallenged. But what of the other professions? How sure is their title? How firm their standards?

Perhaps we ought to examine this word "professional" to obtain a firmer grasp of its meaning and importance. First of all, there is little doubt that the word is of increasing interest and importance in our nation today. As our society becomes more complex, it becomes more professionalized; the proportion of professional men within our population has more than quadrupled within the last century. No title is more sought after, none holds more prestige than that of a profession. Other occupations, such as business, may receive greater income; others, such as entertainment, may receive more public notice; but none has greater prestige.

Those who have studied the sociology of the professions in our country are continually struck by the efforts of fringe occupations to claim professional status. Librarians, insurance salesmen, personnel administrators, city managers, YMCA secretaries, beauticians, accountants, publicity men, investment counselors, and a host of others all make arguments for their professional status, all strive to achieve this magical term of approval and prestige. Practically all of these people are serious and well-intentioned; they genuinely believe that their occupations deserve the term "profession" and also believe, perhaps not incorrectly, that the standards and ideals of those following their occupation will improve if only the term "profession" can be applied.

Any young person contemplating a career today has every reason to ask about its professional status. What, then, about the military occupation? Is the often-used phrase "the military profession" really meaningful? There is little doubt that the military officer's occupation is, at least traditionally, thought of as a profession. For example, the *Oxford Shorter Dictionary*, in defining the word "profession" states, among other things: "Applied specifically to the three learned professions of divinity, law and medicine; also the military profession." Although those military officers who aspire to professional status might look rather gloomily upon their separation from the word "learned" in this definition, the fact remains that a host of other aspirants to the magical term are not even mentioned.

What are the essential characteristics of the professional man? Bernard Barber, a sociologist who has done much work in this field, sees four:

1. A high degree of general and systematic knowledge.
2. Primary orientation to the community interest rather than self-interest.
3. A high degree of self-control of behavior through codes of ethics.
4. A system of rewards, both monetary and honorary, which are primarily symbolic and not means to some end of individual self-interest.

Samuel Huntington, who has written extensively on the professional status of the military, sees three attributes of importance in estimating the professional status of any occupation:

1. Expertise in a significant field of human endeavor.
2. Responsibility to use that expertise in a manner beneficial to the functioning of society.
3. A sense of belonging to a corporate body which stands apart from the layman and at the same time enforces certain standards of competence and conduct.

The basic concepts revealed in these two lists of professional characteristics are similar. Knowledge, responsibility, and self-regulation stand out. The insistence upon knowledge, expertise, competence, learning, or skill in some field not understood by the general public is particularly striking.

However, many occupations can claim special knowledge. The characteristic of responsibility toward the welfare of the community in some significant area of its concern restricts the concept considerably. This is the factor that eliminates the public relations man, the beautician, and others from serious consideration. It also eliminates the professional athlete or the professional entertainer, traditional users of the word "professional" in an altogether different context.

Nevertheless, such occupations as investment counseling and estate planning can make serious claim to highly specialized knowledge and responsibility for vital concerns of the individual; it is the third attribute, that of a recognizable corporate organization which enforces certain standards of competence and conscience upon its practitioners, that narrows the field so severely.

We have then, it appears, three basic concepts: specialized knowledge in some significant field; responsibility to use that knowledge primarily in the interest of others; and membership in a recognized group dedicated to enforcing certain standards and capable of granting meaningful rewards. What of the naval officer's occupation in this light?

It is immediately apparent that to term every naval officer a true professional would be out of the question. A newly commissioned ensign, possessed of a college degree and a few weeks of training in an officer candidate school, possesses no specialized knowledge in a field of significance to the community. His status is not comparable to that of the new doctor, or even to that of the new intern.

On the other hand, to deny that there are officers who possess all of the characteristics we have outlined would also be wrong. One cannot deny that a successful general or admiral serving as, say, one of our unified commanders responsible for command of all United States armed forces over a large geographic area of the world is a professional in the deepest sense of the word. We are forced to conclude that some naval officers are professionals and some are not.

But we must not jump to the conclusion that it is only length of service that makes the difference. Is the officer who has decided to spend his active career in the Navy automatically a professional? I think the answer must be an emphatic no; indeed, the term "professional soldier" connotes the very opposite of some of those attributes we have considered vital.

But if the new ensign is denied the title and it is granted to the admiral holding high command, then where is the dividing line? Does it come suddenly, at some given rank? Before we can answer this question, we must define the essential ingredients of naval professionalism. To begin with, it is apparent that the subject of knowledge, of learning, of expertise, is of great importance. It is perhaps in this area that the military officer is most often challenged in his quest for professional status.

What is it that the admiral knows and the ensign does not? I believe his knowledge can be broken down into four broad categories: sea knowledge, technological competence, command ability, and staff competence.

Sea knowledge is the foundation of the naval profession, and although there are many naval officers who do not possess it, they cannot be considered professional in our sense of the word. Much of this knowledge is mundane, and rarely is it of an intellectual nature. It starts with the sea itself, its characteristics, and its behavior under various conditions of weather; it includes the behavior of ships in the sea, an awareness of what is dangerous and what is not, a knowledge of when to take precautions and how to calculate a risk at sea. It also covers such matters as piloting and navigation, tides and currents, and a capacity to judge where ships can go safely and where not, which waters are minable and which not, where submarines can be expected and where they cannot operate, how ships are handled in formation or when approaching a mooring, in short, all the intrinsic capabilities and limitations of ships.

Some of this sea knowledge is almost folklore, and much of it is shared by rough and uneducated men in many parts of the world in ships of every type and description. Taken alone, it cannot be considered professional knowledge in any learned sense of the word; combined with other elements of military professionalism, it is of the essence.

Our second category, that of technological competence, is a more difficult matter. It has become a commonplace to observe the swiftly growing complexity of modern weapons. How much of the technology involved can we expect a professional naval officer to know? Can the Polaris submarine commanding officer leap, like Walter Mitty, to the side of his non-operating digital computer or nuclear power-plant component and unerringly put his finger on the source of the trouble, repairing it if necessary with a hastily converted part of an old fountain pen? No, not really.

But true professionalism, to say nothing of the successful and safe operation of our modern ships and planes, does require a significant amount of technological knowledge so complex that some very professional officers of the past might have been sorely pressed to meet this requirement. It is necessary, for one thing, to distinguish between operational knowledge and maintenance ability. To know how to start up or turn on equipment, operate it successfully, and turn it off is an altogether different matter from knowing how to repair it, as housewives have been proving with automobiles for decades.

Unlike the housewife, however, the modern naval officer depends upon his highly technical equipment to take him places where not only his own life but the lives of hundreds of his men depend upon its successful operation. It is obvious that his competence to judge whether certain equipment can or cannot operate safely or can or cannot be successfully repaired at sea, affects his ship's safety. Clearly this takes knowledge beyond the turn-it-on, turn-it-off category—and that knowledge alone can become bewilderingly complex with some of our new equipment.

The naval officer of today faces a real challenge in the area of technological competence. The temptation to specialize is strong, and yet the true specialist in technological matters cannot be considered a professional naval officer in our sense. On the other hand, to expect every naval officer to have a complete knowledge of all the Navy's equipment is expecting too much. The field has become too large.

Fortunately, there are common characteristics in many types of modern equipment. A sound knowledge of practical electronics is almost a professional necessity; the fundamental principles of capacitances, inductances, relays, amplifiers, rectifiers, solid-state devices, and cathode-ray applications pervade our Navy today the way rope, tar, and canvas did a century and a half ago. They are part of our professional equipment, and a basic understanding of their principles and applications will go a long way toward explaining the fundamental working of much of our new naval equipment.

More and more, the naval officer must understand the principles of metallurgy in order to make sound judgments about his ships, his planes, his missiles, and their capabilities and limitations. Indeed, the limitations of more and more weapons and vehicles are being determined by this field of knowledge. An understanding of what things can and cannot be safely welded at sea, what machinery may be hastily put into service in an emergency and what must, under any circumstances, be carefully warmed up—these and a host of other matters of importance to a commanding officer often depend upon a basic understanding of metallurgical principles.

In sum, while no one person can be competent in the operation and maintenance of all of the modern Navy's equipment, the professional naval officer needs to be sufficiently well grounded in engineering principles to make sound judgments without relying entirely on the advice and counsel of others.

Our third element of naval professionalism, command ability, like our first, is peculiarly of the sea. Command of a warship at sea is an experience without an exact counterpart in any other occupation. The elements of initiative, judgment, self-reliance, imagination, responsibility, and leadership brought into play here come very close to being unique.

But command of single ships is only a part of the naval officer's required professional command experience. When ships begin to work in company, problems of tactics, communication, and command become complex. Command over groups of ships at sea is a step in the development of the naval professional that requires both a thorough knowledge of the sea itself and of single-ship command.

As the naval officer becomes proficient in broad command at sea, he will inevitably become involved in our fourth level of professional knowledge: that of the staff. Commanders of large numbers of ships and aircraft need assistance in the discharge of their duties, and naval staffs are organized with this in mind. Even more complex, however, is the type of staff required to run our unified commands and joint task forces. The naval officer who would serve usefully in this area must have a knowledge of Army and Air Force organization and theory as well as that prescribed for joint use. A unified command staff or joint task force staff is a complex and intricate affair. Certain groups of these men are expert in supply, transportation, and personnel matters; others in the gathering of intelligence; and still others in the overall task of planning large operations. These are all professional skills, and the naval officer who aspires to professionalism must understand them; they are not peculiar to the sea, but they are increasingly important in the joint command of our armed forces.

These four elements, then, in my view, are the ingredients of naval professionalism. Experience with each is necessary to the whole of professional knowledge. But, even if attained, this knowledge comprises only the first of our three attributes. What of the other two: orientation to community interest and membership in a corporate body capable of self-control and the dispensing of rewards?

In regard to its orientation to the community interest, there is not much that need be said about the naval officer's occupation. It has no other aim. It is entirely devoted to the protection and furtherance of the national community; those of its members who use it for other purposes have, by definition, divested themselves of any claim to professionalism.

Let us pass on to the third characteristic, membership in a corporate body of useful and significant powers. Our best hope in this area is to trace the evolution of those institutions which give the naval profession its distinguishing characteristics today: its ability to select its own leaders, its provision of adequate procurement and retirement procedures, the development of its schools and colleges, its achievement of an intellectual credo, and its evolution of those ideals and aspirations which separate a profession from other means of earning a livelihood. A profession must have a history; by its very nature, it is evolved, not created at one fell swoop.

Let us turn briefly to the pages of American naval history and attempt to identify those events which have been important in the evolution of an American naval profession.

Although it is difficult to pick a precise date, the year 1842 makes a convenient starting point from which to trace the evolution of the naval profession.

Before this time, the Navy had not varied much from the days of 1775, when John Adams drew the first "rules for the government of the American Navy" by modifying only slightly the King's Regulations and Admiralty Instructions of 1772. The sailing ship was the Navy, and by 1842 its form had gone essentially unchanged for nearly two centuries. Although our Navy had fought actions in both the Revolution and the War of 1812 which were classics of gallantry and seamanship, the naval profession, in our sense of the word, did not exist.

Boys learned to be officers by going to sea as midshipmen and growing up in a school of hard knocks hardly designed to produce anything but pragmatic skills. There was no organized system of promotion and retirement. Officers moved up the ladder of rank only as men died off at the top. The simple system of seniority was the new democracy's answer to the threat of favoritism in the appointment of officers, but it resulted in a dreadful stagnation of promotion. By mid-nineteenth century, of the 68 captains on active duty, the youngest was fifty-six; the 327 lieutenants ranged in age from thirty to fifty; and some of the midshipmen were still waiting for promotion to officer rank when they were thirty-seven.

Naval technology consisted mainly of splicing rope and tarring seams. The Navy had no overall concept of its strategic purpose, it had no permanent school for the training of its officers, and if there were enforceable standards of professional conduct in the corps, they were not overly evident. The reputation of book-learning among the officers was low, dueling was still prevalent, and the tot of rum with the threat of the lash played a large part in the leadership program on board most of the ships of the 1842 Navy.

It has been said that the armed forces of a particular nation are about as good as the nation wants and deserves. This is perhaps another way of observing that these forces are inevitably a reflection of the society they serve. In the mid-nineteenth century, with the nation half a century old, a revolution in manners, morals, education, and labor practices began which was in many ways a counterpart of the political revolution of 1776. Its effect upon the Navy was profound.

In the growth of concern for the welfare of the individual which began to sweep the nation about this time, attention was focused on the conditions under which men lived at sea. A young Harvard student named Richard Henry Dana shipped in the merchant marine as an ordinary seaman in order to obtain a prescribed rest for his failing eyesight. Upon his return to Cambridge, he described his experiences in *Two Years before the Mast*, a book which aroused the conscience of the nation. Dana's vivid descriptions of the flogging of sailors spread-eagled against the shrouds of a sailing ship made the nation aware of what was going on aboard its ships. This was not the Navy, but everyone knew that flogging was still practiced in the Navy—and public opinion was rising against it.

Over the protests of some naval officers, who feared for the maintenance of shipboard discipline without it, but with the wholehearted support of others, Congress, in 1850, prohibited flogging in the Navy. For a short period after the abolition there were indeed some serious disciplinary troubles. Desertions increased, and many good sailors, feeling that a man's punishment was a man's right, refused to reenlist in a service they felt was being spoiled by the do-gooders from New England. However, before long, provisions were made for holding summary courts-martial on board ship so that offenses could be punished by reduction in rating, loss of pay, performance of extra duties, and other reasonable measures. Discipline gradually returned, and the crunch of the cat on bare flesh was never again part of the scene in the American Navy.

The same wave of humanitarian concern that abolished flogging soon affected another fixture of Navy life—the sailor's daily ration of grog. From the earliest days, the allowance per man had been half a pint per day, with the allowance doubled on Christmas. In 1842, the Secretary of the Navy had yielded to the New England influence to the extent of cutting the grog allowance in half and prohibiting it to minors. Still, the cargo of whisky on a forty-four-gun frigate amounted to one hundred barrels, and was the largest single item of expense for the stores of the ship. The New Englanders persisted, and just as the Civil War was beginning, Congress passed an act stating that the "spirit ration in the navy of the United States shall forever cease."

The departure of flogging and grog, while perhaps not of overwhelming importance in itself, was tangible evidence of a change within the society and, thus, within the men of the Navy. The rights of individuals—the recognition of the hopes and aspirations of each member of the crew, no matter how humble his station—were beginning to be a matter of national concern. The political principles on which the nation was founded were beginning to go into practice, and it was inevitable that a different sort of officer corps would be required.

The story of the *Somers* mutiny has already been related, but its occurrence at about this time heightened the feeling that at least one step which had long been needed must at last be undertaken. The establishment of the Naval Academy at Annapolis in 1845, although a crude and elementary beginning, marked a crucial early step in the formation of the naval profession.

As is usually the case, there was a complex variety of pressures at work upon the Navy in this decade of the 1840s; the winds of change were blowing in quarters other than those concerned with social matters. By 1835 the transatlantic steamship was a success, and there were nearly 700 steam craft of one sort or another in use on the inland and coastal waters of the United States. Still, except for a brief experiment with a steam-driven harbor-defense battery during the War of 1812, the Navy had not built a single steam warship. Finally, in June of 1837, at the New York Navy Yard, the steam frigate *Fulton* was launched and began to fit out for her sea trials. She was widely regarded with suspicion and mistrust.

Beyond the fact that the steamship was attempting to displace a fighting machine which had been in existence almost unchanged for two centuries, there was an emotional block in the path of the steamship which is hard to define but nevertheless understandable. There is something poetic, an atmosphere of grace and beauty, an economy of means, and a sort of mystique, about a sailing ship. Its very appearance and feel as it leans with the wind and surges through the sea, the salty tang of the language used to describe its parts and control its workings—all of these things have caught the imagination and emotions of men for centuries. Was all this beauty and utility to come tumbling down before the dirty, clanging steam engine? It was too much for all but a gifted few to see and understand.

In addition to the emotional blocks, there were real drawbacks to the new mode of power. Fuel was not available on the distant patrol stations then being manned by the Navy; sail was the only practical means by which the long cruises could be made. In addition, the paddle wheels of the early steamships harmed their sailing characteristics and were obviously vulnerable to gunfire, as was the steam machinery itself. The weight of all the machinery demanded a reduction in the number of guns which could be carried on a ship of given size. All these objections were raised, along with such questions as: will Congress appropriate the money for these much-more-expensive ships? How can we supply the spare parts that will be needed for repairs on distant stations? And where can we get the highly trained men required to operate and maintain the engines at sea?

The *Fulton* was not an unqualified success, but she began to impose important changes on the Navy from the first. It was clear that a group of trained officers who understood the new engines would be required, and in 1842 the corps of engineers was established; this corps gave the line officer the first serious challenge to his authority and prestige. The same year saw the creation of the Navy's bureau system, which remains to this day the foundation of its technological organization.

Secretary of the Navy George Bancroft was responsible for important changes within the Navy other than the establishment of the Naval Academy. Turning his attention to officer promotion, he was appalled at what he saw. The lack of a retirement plan coupled with the seniority system clogged the rolls of the Navy with ancient mariners who were no longer physically capable of going to sea. The Secretary had no choice but to order able-bodied younger officers to duty in the ships and allow the oldsters, with their relatively high rank, to luxuriate in shore jobs or be sent on permanent leave with half pay. In the meantime, they blocked the promotion of all below.

Bancroft wrote to the Chairman of the House Naval Affairs Committee: "I hope you are friendly to a retired list and to the young officers of the Navy. The present system puts upon the active all the hazard and toil, and gives promotions and emoluments to the idlers at home."

Although he was not able to bring it about during his own administration, Bancroft's efforts eventually bore fruit. In 1855, the President appointed a board of fifteen naval officers to make an investigation into the efficiency of officers of the line and report to the Secretary of the Navy those who were "incapable of performing promptly and efficiently all their duties both ashore and afloat."

What President Pierce had actually done was to appoint, in effect, the first naval selection board. Significantly, it consisted only of naval officers, and they were to decide who, within their own ranks, did not meet the standards of the Navy. Here, indeed, was the beginning of a professional attribute. Selection boards did not become a permanent and accepted institution of the Navy for many years, but the board of 1855 was important as a beginning.

As a beginning, it was spectacular. The board deliberated for some five weeks and then found 201 line officers—roughly a quarter of all those on active duty—incompetent for further service. It recommended 49 for dismissal and the remainder for retirement. Few events in the professional history of the Navy have shaken it the way this board report did. To many of the Navy's older officers, the changes of the 1840s, such as the advent of steam, the establishment of an Academy ashore, and the abolition of flogging and grog, were abundant evidence that the Navy was rapidly going downhill to a remote and hot location. However, the board of 1855 was something else again—it was not just evidence of moral decay, it threw them out of a job. The uproar was magnificent.

The press, the Congress, the church, and every other institution that could be pressed into service took up the cry. The *Scientific American* stated that the board had smitten every officer in the Navy who had accomplished anything in the scientific line, and the State Legislature of New Jersey sent a formal resolution to the board complaining that the ranking officer of the Navy, a sterling native son of New Jersey, had been ruthlessly stricken with the rest.

President Pierce did his best to hold the line against such aroused public opinion and, apparently, he did reasonably well. In any event, the controversy was soon to be forgotten in the heat of emotions of a larger sort which were already dividing the nation and sounding the drums of war.

Important institutional changes in military professionalism rarely come during the conduct of wars; they are more frequent in the wake of such events. Occasionally, as in the reforms of the 1840s, they come just before. We must search the pages of history until well after the Civil War before we find further significant progress.

We have already spoken of Stephen B. Luce in connection with his service to the post–Civil War Naval Academy. This officer, who entered the Navy as a midshipman in 1841, was to make an enormous contribution to naval professionalism before the end of the century. During the Civil War, Luce worked with General William T. Sherman to plan Army–Navy cooperation for the movement into South Carolina. He was impressed with Sherman's professionalism and with the orderly thought processes which Sherman applied to the creation of military plans. Luce began to see that some of the same principles applied to naval planning. Was it possible that there were underlying principles in naval warfare that had not yet been identified and set forth in print? The idea was to absorb much of Luce's thinking in later years.

It was apparent to Luce from the outset that what he was thinking about was an intellectual task. This sort of thing had simply been outside the framework of naval experience up to that time. Clausewitz and Jomini had undertaken such work for the armies of the world, but who could do it for the Navy? Luce knew of no one capable of the task but he continued to ponder the question.

In the meantime, he concerned himself with the advancement of learning and professional activity within the Navy. In 1873, he was one of the leaders in the foundation of the Naval Institute, the purpose of which was, and remains to this day, to advance "professional and scientific knowledge in the Navy." A year later the Institute began to publish its Proceedings, which since that time have acted as a useful forum of professional expression for the Navy. Fittingly, the entire first issue of the Institute Proceedings was devoted to an article by Luce.

His mind, however, continued to be occupied with the formalization and expression of naval principles of war and strategy. In 1883, Luce wrote a personal letter to the Secretary of the Navy urging the establishment of a "war school" for naval officers. As a result of this letter, the Secretary appointed a board, of which Luce was chairman, to study the matter. The report of the board stated, in part:

> The Board is of the opinion that a cogent reason for such a school is that there may be a place where our officers will not only be encouraged, but required to study their profession proper—war—in a far more thorough manner than has ever heretofore been attempted, and to bring to the investigation of the various problems of modern naval warfare the scientific methods adopted in other professions.

The Secretary was persuaded, and shortly thereafter issued the General Order which established the Naval War College at Newport. Appropriately, Luce was the first president.

In his search for instructors for his college, Luce wrote to an acquaintance who at the time was commanding a small steam sloop in South American waters. He invited the officer to lecture on naval history and tactics, and with his acceptance a chain of events was set in motion that profoundly affected the fate of the United States Navy and had not a little influence on world history. The officer's name was Alfred Thayer Mahan.

Luce's letter to Mahan told him that one of his tasks at Newport would be to trace the course of naval history in a search for general principles showing the causes of success and failure in war. Mahan's reply made it clear that he would like to accept the assignment but would require considerable time to prepare himself for the task. This was something of an understatement. Although Mahan accepted the position in September of 1884 and the War College commenced operation in September of 1885, Mahan did not actually report to Newport until August of 1886. He had not, however, been idle. He had retained command of his ship for most of the first year, much of which time he was able to spend in study. He devoted most of the remaining time to reading the history of the world's naval campaigns in the Astor Place branch of the New York Public Library.

During all of this time, Mahan was shaping a concept in which he saw naval power as an agent of history and one of the major factors in the creation of national power. He began his lecture course at Newport in the fall of 1886, and by 1890 the lectures had crystallized sufficiently to be published in book form.

In *The Influence of Sea Power upon History*, Mahan limited himself to only slightly more than a century of time: he started with 1660, the date when the sailing ship era could be said to have fairly begun, and closed with 1783, the end of the American Revolution. Within this period of some 120 years Mahan examined, in his own words, ". . . the general history of Europe and America with particular reference to the effect of sea power upon the course of that history."

It was of pivotal importance that Mahan did not confine himself to a recitation of the sea battles of that period, but rather looked upon the whole sweep of history with an attempt to determine how the use of the sea had affected it. No one had done this before; the professional historians had more or less ignored the sea, and the naval historians were only chroniclers of battles. When Mahan bridged the two, he broke important new ground.

Perhaps wisely, he put the essence of his message in the first chapter of his more-than-500-page book. Herein he set forth the three great links in the creation of sea power: internal strength, a merchant marine protected by an adequate navy, and possession of overseas colonies at locations strategic both for the support of the merchant marine and for the purposes of war. He concluded his great first chapter with a discussion of how his own country had failed to develop and maintain the last two links in the chain.

This was heady wine in the world of 1890, when not only the United States but also the rapidly growing industrial nations of Germany and Japan were beginning to flex their muscles and wonder if ever they could equal the brilliance and power of Great Britain. The book's impact was perhaps greater overseas than at home; it was translated and read in most of the capitals and admiralties of the world. Needless to say, the Royal Navy itself took up Mahan avidly, and when, in a subsequent book on the Napoleonic wars and Nelson, he wrote, "Those far-distant, storm-beaten ships upon which the Grand Army never looked, stood between it and dominion of the world," the British Navy knew that it had found an advocate more skillful and eloquent than any it had developed at home.

Woven through Mahan's two books on sea power was a concept of naval strategy which was really the fruit for which Luce had been searching since his first meeting with Sherman. It had to do with the relationship of commerce-raiding and blockading to the primary purpose of a navy in war. Commerce-raiding was the preoccupation of the American Navy during much of the Revolution and the War of 1812, while blockading had been its principal task in the Civil War. Mahan saw these efforts as violations of the principle of concentration of force which he, along with Clausewitz and Jomini, saw as one of the maxims of war.

Although he did not condemn commerce-raiding and blockading as secondary operations, he held that the primary task of a navy in war was to concentrate its fighting ships in sufficient force to defeat any fleet the enemy could reasonably assemble, seek out enemy warships and defeat them, and thus gain control of the seas. Mahan held that if the battle fleet dominated the high seas, coastal defense was unnecessary, blockading a simple matter, and commerce-raiding a matter to be done at leisure. Conversely, and perhaps more important to the United States, if the navy of a nation were constructed and trained only for commerce-raiding, then that nation itself would be vulnerable to blockade because it could not genuinely control the seas. Mahan pointed out that the Navy of the United States had, in his opinion, just that weakness.

The influence of Mahan's book on the affairs of his own Navy was direct and immediate. The new administration of Benjamin Harrison was anxious to push naval construction, and Secretary of the Navy Benjamin Tracy's first annual report to Congress in 1889 sounded as though it might have been written by Mahan himself. (Perhaps it was.) Indeed, later editions of Mahan's book contained a footnote stating, "Since the above was written, the Secretary of the Navy, in his report for 1889, has recommended a fleet which would make such a blockade . . . very hazardous."

The events of the Spanish–American War seemed living vindication of the words of Mahan. Theodore Roosevelt, an avid reader of Mahan, was Assistant Secretary of the Navy when the war began. With the attention of the world centered on Cuba and the sinking of the *Maine*, the young Roosevelt had been quietly at work assembling and equipping a suitable naval striking force on the other side of the world in Hong Kong. When war was declared in late April of 1898, the ships were ready to sail.

In the early dawn of May 1, Commodore Dewey entered Manila Harbor with his ships and in a few hours reduced the Spanish fleet of Admiral Montojo to ruins. Dewey promptly warned the Spanish Governor General at Manila that another shot from the shore batteries would result in the destruction of the city. The governor gave up, and Dewey anchored his flagship close enough to the newly silenced ramparts so that the citizens of Manila could hear the strains of the evening concert played by the ship's band. Fittingly, it consisted mainly of Spanish music. It all proved too much for the colonel commanding the shore battery, who ended the day by shooting himself.

The news of the victory was received with hysterical delight at home. Overnight, Dewey became a popular hero, and those who had read Mahan's book marveled at the way Roosevelt had made its words take life. Were the Philippines to become the first building block in a new empire, this time American?

When, only a short time later, Sampson knocked Spanish sea power from the Atlantic with his victory at Santiago, Cuba, the demonstration of the Mahan theory seemed complete. With the United States controlling the oceans, Spain was helpless to pursue the war further, either in Cuba or in the Philippines.

It is not easy to put Mahan in proper perspective. The condition of the nation and the course of world events which surrounded the publication of his first books make it difficult to determine how much of what happened resulted from Mahan's work and how much would have happened anyway. At the very least, his work was a genuinely scholarly effort which drew from its examination of history a theory of world power very much in tune with the times.

More difficult to evaluate is the theory of naval strategy which evolved from his study of history. It has suffered much from over-publicizing and under-reading. There has been a regrettable tendency to represent Mahan as a sort of high priest of the naval profession who left a record of divinely revealed, immutable principles concerning war on the sea. This is not fair to a scholarly, earnest man who attempted only to express the principles of sea power as he saw them in his time and in the context of the weapons then available.

The development of the submarine and the airplane both introduced new dimensions into naval warfare, and made it a far more complex matter than it had been in 1890. Modern political alliances have also significantly changed the world environment in which Mahan developed his overseas-base theory.

The important point is that with the publication of Mahan's books, the long drought of professional material on the principles of sea power had been broken. New weapons and new diplomatic developments would bring new theories and new books; Mahan's contribution to the naval profession was not an eternal set of truths written on golden plates but rather a convincing demonstration that the subject of sea power is worthy of careful and deliberate academic analysis and expression.

Seen in this light, Mahan and his work stand as one of the milestones in the establishment of an American naval profession. Never a great operational officer at sea, Mahan demonstrated to his fellow officers the importance of theory to their calling. No occupation can aspire to be called a profession without men who pursue, and attempt to identify in writing, the theories behind its actual practice.

As a profession must have its theorists, so must it have its practical leaders—men of vision like the theorists, but men who concentrate more on action than on principles.

Such a man began to emerge from the shadows of the naval officer corps soon after the end of the Spanish War. In 1901, in Hong Kong, there occurred a meeting that was to have long consequences for the United States Navy. There, a strikingly handsome and forceful American lieutenant named William Sowden Sims met Captain Sir Percy Scott of the Royal Navy. Scott, a brilliant but controversial officer, clearly understood what the arrival of the steam-and-steel warship meant to the naval profession. The new ships with their long-range rifled guns firing explosive shells were delicate pieces of machinery, capable of much higher performance than they were actually delivering under the training practices then in use. Scott saw that an altogether different plateau of organization and personnel training was required if these new ships were to realize their potential.

As a first order of business, they had to learn to shoot better. Scott developed a new method of aiming and firing his guns known as the continuous-aim system. Previously, naval gunners had fired their weapons when the roll of the ship brought the sights on the target; in large ships this roll can be a ponderous movement taking relatively long periods of time. Employing a telescopic sight invented by United States Navy Lieutenant Bradley Fiske (of whom we shall hear more later) as well as a faster gun-laying mechanism, Scott produced a system whereby the gunner could keep on the target throughout the roll of the ship.

Sims saw immediately the advantages of such a system, both

in accuracy and in rate of fire. Further, he was convinced American naval gunnery needed improvement. For all its fine performance in the Spanish War, the Navy's gunnery had been poor. Sims took up the battle like a missionary spreading the gospel. He talked and wrote practically nothing but the continuous-aim system; hits-per-gun-per-minute became his byword and he began to bombard the Bureau of Ordnance with letters demanding changes in the fleet's gunnery installations.

Sims was fighting some great obstacles. A sort of mystique grows up around the large guns of the Navy, and the men who served them on board the ships of 1901 were not anxious to change their time-honored methods on the word of some lieutenant they did not know, no matter how persuasive and handsome he might be. Similarly, those in Washington responsible for ordnance were perfectly satisfied with the mounts and sights then installed, and to make expensive alterations to suit the whims of a lieutenant who kept writing from the far reaches of the Pacific did not strike them as necessary. Their files were full of such stuff, they would say wearily as they closed their offices for another day.

But this was no ordinary lieutenant. He gave early indication of this by addressing one of his letters to Theodore Roosevelt, newly arrived in the White House as a result of McKinley's assassination. The letter was a serious breach of propriety in those days—as it would be today—but there is considerable evidence that Sims, who had never met the President at the time, understood the gravity of what he was doing and sincerely considered the state of the Navy's gunnery serious enough to justify hazarding his career.

In any event, the letter gave facts and figures about the Navy's gunnery accuracy and made an eloquent case for changes. Roosevelt did not, as legend has it, immediately call Sims home from the Orient to straighten out the gunnery situation, but he did send Sims a sympathetic reply, and on some later occasions Roosevelt was of direct help to Sims.

Considerably later, Sims was ordered to the Bureau of Navigation to become Inspector of Target Practice for the Navy. He used the office in vigorous style. He toured the fleet, gave lectures, wrote letters, and levied criticism (not all of it justified) with such vigor that he succeeded in antagonizing many fine and dedicated officers. Overall, however, he made an enormous contribution. Complacency is one of the great peacetime hazards of the naval profession, and no one could feel very complacent when Sims was around. He took both criticism and praise with the feeling that his job was uppermost. When he left the Office of Inspector in 1908, it could truthfully be said that he had, almost single-handed, revolutionized American naval gunnery and brought it to a foremost position among the navies of the world.

Sims' six years in the gunnery fight gave him some strong ideas on the need for a Navy line staff in Washington. Although the Navy's material bureaus had been established in the nation's capital since 1842, the line officers of the Navy were essentially without representation in Washington. This is not to say that the aims and interests of the bureaus were different from those of the line, but theirs was inevitably a different viewpoint. Although occasionally officers with seagoing backgrounds were assigned to the bureaus, they were more commonly manned by staff officers (engineering, supply, medical, and so on) and by civilian officials of long tenure.

Everyone concerned wanted what was best for the Navy, but there was often disagreement as to just what was best. The seagoing officers lacked a base in Washington from which to express their views. The Bureau of Navigation had been turned into a sort of line-officers' establishment, but it lacked any authority over the other bureaus. It was clear to Sims that only when he got to Washington was he able to exert the leverage to get big reforms made; and even then, he was continually handicapped by limitations on the legal authority of the Navy's line officers.

Significantly, at the same time that Sims was engaged in his gunnery struggles, Elihu Root, Theodore Roosevelt's great Secretary of War, was conducting his fight to obtain a general staff for the Army. Citing the often-confused logistic and intelligence situations in the Spanish War as evidence, Root succeeded in establishing a staff system for the Army in which the Chief of Staff and his immediate assistants were placed in authority not only over the troops in the field but over the support branches (equivalent of the Navy's bureaus) of the Army. Sims immediately saw what such an organization could do for the Navy, and he, as well as a number of his contemporaries, started demanding a similar system.

Sims received strong support from President Roosevelt but was not successful. The Army's example did not clear the way for Sims. Army officers themselves had not urged the Root reforms—indeed, they had opposed them. The sight of the eloquent and opinionated Sims, with his strongly magnetic personality, urging a measure that would give the naval officers of the line unprecedented authority in Washington may have killed whatever chances President Roosevelt had of obtaining congressional support for such a system for the Navy. In any event, with the end of Roosevelt's second term, Sims thought he saw the end of hope for the staff reforms, and left Washington for sea duty.

The new administration of William Howard Taft brought help from an unexpected quarter when Secretary of the Navy George Meyer set up a board of line officers to supervise the work of the bureaus. The concept, however, never received the approval of Congress. When Meyer left office on the election of Woodrow Wilson, the line board largely disappeared and the fight for a staff resumed about where it had left off when Taft took office.

Woodrow Wilson appointed Josephus Daniels, a North Carolina newspaper editor, as Secretary of the Navy. A man of deep patriotic sentiments and sincere humanitarian interests, Daniels did not altogether understand the nature of the Navy at first, nor the crisis in which it found itself with the approach of war. One of the remnants of the Meyer system was a rear admiral who served as the Secretary's aide for operations. The officer occupying this post was Bradley Fiske, the same man who had invented the telescopic gunsight (of such importance to Sims and his gunnery reforms) as well as a number of other devices of significance—the torpedo plane is only one example. Fiske was a highly professional and loyal officer who found himself deeply concerned that the new Secretary did not understand the nature of the task ahead of the Navy.

Fiske wrote several memoranda concerning the need for a staff of line officers in Washington to make war plans, allocate resources, and eventually supervise the conduct of the war at sea. Daniels remained unpersuaded, and Fiske eventually became so concerned with the situation that he felt it necessary to violate his professional ethics and circumvent his civilian superior. Fiske realized that with the approach of war, the support of Congress could be obtained if only the case were properly made. Testifying before the House in December of 1914, Fiske argued the case for a staff of line officers similar to that provided for the Army under the Elihu Root reforms of 1903. His testimony was so effective that it was only a short time before a bill was drafted to create a Chief of Naval Operations with a staff of not less than fifteen officers to be "responsible for the readiness of the Navy for war and be charged with its general direction." In effect, this would have given the Navy the vertical system, like that of the Army, that Sims had advocated.

Secretary Daniels, understandably enough, objected strenuously to the testimony of his aide and to the proposed legislation. He succeeded in having the bill altered to delete the staff of fifteen assistants and, more important, to state that the Chief of Naval Operations "shall, *under the direction of the Secretary of the Navy*, be charged with the operations of the fleet, and with the preparation and readiness of plans for its use in war." Authority over the material bureaus was not mentioned. Thus, in effect, was created the parallel (or bilineal) organization which had been advocated by Luce and Mahan rather than the vertical system of the Army.

The next year (1916) the Office of the Chief of Naval Operations was significantly strengthened when the fifteen assistants were restored, the rank of the office was established as full admiral, and it was made clear that orders issued by the Chief of Naval Operations "shall be considered as emanating from the Secretary." The bilineal system, however, remained. Thus the struggle of the line for a place of power within the Navy Department ended in a useful compromise.

It is most difficult to pass objective judgment on these strongly felt conflicts of half a century ago. Certainly Bradley Fiske violated a fundamental precept of his profession when he challenged the authority of his civilian superior. Did the end justify the means? Whatever the correct judgment, Fiske paid a heavy price. Daniels never forgave the disloyalty of his aide, and before long Fiske found it necessary to resign from his post and from active service.

Whatever might be said of the unorthodox moves which Sims, Fiske, and others of the naval profession made, time has not proved them wrong in their basic aim. The Office of the Chief of Naval Operations has served the Navy—and many Secretaries of the Navy—well, through half a century and two world wars. Its creation was a logical necessity as the Navy grew in complexity and size; no one can say whether or not the changes would have come with less direct and vigorous action on the part of Fiske.

Suffice it to say that at the peak of an extraordinarily useful career, he had the courage to sacrifice his personal position for what he thought was in the best interests of the nation.

Lest we leave our discussion of Josephus Daniels on an uncertain note, let us turn our attention to the Naval Act of 1916, one of the most important pieces of legislation in our history from the professional point of view. This act, which provided for the construction of a significant number of warships, also created the Naval Aviation Corps, established a naval reserve organization, and instituted the officer-selection and promotion system which remains the basis of that in use today. The foundations of the modern Navy were laid in the Naval Act of 1916—and much of the credit for its construction and passage must go to Josephus Daniels, as well as to his Assistant Secretary of the Navy, a promising young man named Franklin Delano Roosevelt.

The officer-promotion law of 1916 provided for annual selection boards to be made up of officers senior to those being screened for advancement. These boards were to choose, from among those eligible by length of service, the officers to be promoted to the next higher rank. An allowed percentage of the total number of officers was established for each rank, which provided a pyramid-shaped structure in which number diminished as seniority increased. Flow through this constantly narrowing structure was forced by considering a new crop of officers for each rank each year. An officer failing of selection for two years was involuntarily retired from active duty with a pension appropriate to his length of service.

The entire line of the Navy was arranged in a lineal list of seniority; it was this tabulation (published annually) which provided the key to the promotion system. The yearly selection for each rank concerned itself with that segment of the lineal list designated by the Secretary of the Navy as the Promotion Zone. The percentage selection to be followed by the board was also established by the Secretary of the Navy. The staff corps held separate selection boards, but their pace of promotion was locked to that of the line by a system in which each staff corps officer was assigned a particular line officer as his running mate. When the line officer came up for promotion, so did his staff running mate.

A personnel-promotion system to handle the needs of an organization the size of the Navy must necessarily be complex. The description I have given, while not complete, outlines the essential elements of a system which, although modified, persists in the Navy to the present time.

It is not perfect; the appraisal of men by other men is a subjective affair, and good legislation and good will cannot create Solomons. Still, when all criticism is levied and acknowledged, the Act of 1916 provided the naval profession with a singularly fair system of promotion. It has attracted world-wide attention and has been adopted in modified form by many organizations, both in and out of the military, which have need of a fair and efficient system for preventing stagnation in the channels of promotion.

The Naval Act of 1916 was the last in the chain of events beginning before the Civil War which I have identified as central to the establishment of a naval profession in America. True, there have been important events since, but these are the developments which can be said to have molded the naval profession in a corporate sense, and to have given it those capabilities of self-perpetuation and self-regulation characteristic of professions in our initial discussion.

In reviewing these developments, we are impressed with the

momentum which developed throughout this period. The early reforms, such as the abolition of flogging and grog, the introduction of the steamship, and indeed, even the establishment of the Naval Academy, were the work of men outside the naval officer corps. However, with the growing sense of corporateness and professional awareness which came in later years, the reforms began to come from the officers themselves. Luce, Mahan, and Sims did their work in isolation from significant civilian support. The Naval Institute, the Naval War College at Newport, the writings of Mahan, the gunnery reforms, and establishment of the Chief of Naval Operations were all the results of efforts made by naval officers to expand the usefulness of their service. They were clear evidence of a sense of corporateness that meets the requirements of our definition.

By 1916 the naval profession existed. Admission to its ranks was not then—and is even less so today—controlled as sharply and clearly as admission to the professions of law and medicine. No long professional school, no internship, no bar examinations regulate the commissioning of a United States naval officer. It would be impractical and unwise to create such a system. The Navy must always be ready for short-notice expansion, and the commissioning of thousands of new officers overnight is an eventuality for which it must always be prepared.

Nevertheless, the profession exists, even by the rather rigorous definition we accepted at the beginning of this chapter. Its achievement is a long road, its ideals and aspirations too much to ask of many. But like a shore dimly seen, it looms ahead as a possibility for every young officer who would seek it with dedication to its high principles.

CHAPTER SEVEN

What Are the Navy's Traditions?

In the opening years of this century, in Paris, the American Ambassador to France was engaged in a strange search. He was looking for an eighteenth-century Protestant cemetery reputed to hold the grave of John Paul Jones, who had died in that city, unnoticed and almost a pauper, in 1792. In the nearly one hundred years that had gone by since Jones' death, the city had overgrown the cemetery and its location was uncertain. The markers were gone and ordinary buildings covered the site.

Finally, in 1905, a lead coffin was opened to disclose a corpse, preserved in alcohol, which bore a remarkable resemblance to portraits and busts of Jones. Reliable records indicated that a far-sighted French official had paid to have Jones' corpse so preserved on the chance that America might some day wish to reclaim her naval hero. When autopsy by French surgeons uncovered evidence that indicated beyond reasonable doubt that the body was actually that of John Paul Jones, President Theodore Roosevelt dispatched four cruisers to Cherbourg to bring the admiral home. Elaborate ceremonies were held, both in France and in the United States when the body arrived. In April of 1906 the body was placed in a temporary brick vault at Annapolis to await final disposition.

Although Congress delayed for longer than might seem necessary, in January of 1913, the body of John Paul Jones was placed to final rest in the crypt of the Naval Academy chapel in a marble sarcophagus reminiscent of the tomb of Napoleon in Paris' *Les Invalides*—the building which itself had furnished the inspiration for the chapel dome. Although the tomb is elaborate, the inscription on the floor is simple: "He gave our Navy its earliest traditions of heroism and victory." It is not without significance that the interest in locating the body of Jones and returning it to the United States coincided with the upsurge of professional feeling which, as we have seen, occurred during these years.

Professions must have traditions, and the return of Jones to America was only one manifestation of the growing awareness of naval tradition that marked this era. No longer were the buildings of the Academy to bear such quaint names as the Abbey, Brandywine, and Rowdy Row. Instead, Ernest Flagg's new structures were to be titled in memory of Bancroft, Mahan, Sampson, and other heroes of the century just past. The profession was coming of age.

All professions must have traditions, but to no other profession are these traditions more important than they are to the military. Although we have focused on the intellectual dimensions of the naval officer's lot in order to explain this often-neglected area, the fundamental purpose of the Navy remains the use of force in the defense of the nation. In short, it exists to fight.

The actual fighting of wars, as opposed to the theory thereof, is not an intellectual endeavor. Men so engaged do not often respond to arguments of reason and intelligence which might possess great force in other contexts.

This is not to say that American fighting men do not want to know for what they fight, and why. But there must be more than this to persuade men to charge across enemy beaches in the face of withering machine-gun fire, to nose over their airplanes in screaming dives against the black puffs of anti-aircraft fire, or to continue to serve the guns in badly damaged and sinking ships. Why do men do such things when every instinct of self-preservation cries against it? Teamwork, love of country, sheer bravery, the example of a good leader close at hand, fear of later ridicule, fear of letting one's comrades down—a hundred different forces work on men in battle; but tradition is certainly one of the most powerful.

Tradition is inspiring, it enriches our lives, it helps us to understand the purpose of our nation and our Navy—but it is also of concrete value in battle. Americans have always fought well—on the land and on the sea as well as later in the air. The record is a long and essentially unblemished one; those who bear their nation's arms also bear the responsibility of the tradition. Courage, bravery, honor, and heroism are not the words of the classroom. Indeed, they are sometimes scorned from the comfortable perspectives of peace. But when the tocsin of war sounds, they become essential to our survival, and tradition leads them back to the forefront of men's thoughts.

Note that we speak of tradition, not of custom. Custom is the etiquette of a profession, important as courtesy and manners are important to our daily lives. But tradition, in our sense, is a prime mover. Perhaps Joseph Conrad expressed the idea best when he wrote: "The worth of a sentiment lies in the sacrifices men will make for its sake. All ideals are built on the ground of solid achievement, which in a given profession creates in the course of time a certain tradition, or in other words, a standard of conduct." Note the word "achievement"; tradition is the result of achievement by men in the past. Such accomplishments may, of course, occur in peacetime; but the greatest makers of naval tradition have accomplished their works in war. The pursuits of peace have other forces which drive men to their accomplishment; it is war, with its irrational and terrifying situations, which must have the glowing examples of bravery and fortitude from the past. Here tradition pays its way.

It is no empty boast to say that John Paul Jones gave our Navy its earliest traditions of heroism and victory. No one can read Samuel Eliot Morison's account of Jones' desperate action with the British *Serapis* in 1779 without realizing that here was truly one of the great fighting men of the sea. Outgunned, outmanned, and with his supposed ally, the *Alliance*, firing more rounds at him than at the *Serapis*, Jones won the battle by sheer guts and determination. For three and a half hours he engaged in the wildest sort of slugging match at pointblank range and, finally, with *Bonhomme Richard's* rudder hanging by one pintle, her stern frames almost shot away, and several feet of water in the hold, Jones carried the day as the British captain tore down the red ensign with his own hands.

Without delay, Jones gallantly returned the proffered sword of the defeated Englishman and invited him down to his wretched cabin for a glass of wine. This is the stuff of tradition. Although many apocryphal stories about Jones exist (most of them now, fortunately, neatly skewered by Admiral Morison), there is little doubt about the authenticity of the *Serapis* fight. The battle often hangs by a narrow thread, and on many an occasion an apparent defeat has been turned into victory by the stubborn determination of one man. Jones' victory over the *Serapis* remains one of the great examples.

The deeds of the Navy in battle are great reading. Anyone, in or out of the Navy, who wants to understand this venerable American institution must read its record of achievement in the shaping of our nation.

We cannot, in the confines of this book on the naval profession, attempt to present a useful history of the Navy. The job has been well done by many others. Those new to the field may find Fletcher Pratt's histories interesting and useful, particularly for the Navy up to the end of the nineteenth century. Those who want reading in more depth should turn to some of the books on individual naval figures; Elting Morison's book on Sims is one of the best, and Samuel Eliot Morison's *John Paul Jones* is another.

For the officer or prospective officer looking ahead to the 1970s and 1980s, however, the period of greatest interest is that of World War II. The Navy was extraordinarily fortunate to have the great Harvard historian Samuel Eliot Morison willing to undertake the task of writing a naval history of this conflict. His fifteen-volume work on the Navy in World War II stands as one of the finest and most readable serious histories extant. Those who find the length of this work forbidding should note that Admiral Morison has consolidated his fifteen volumes into one, *The Two Ocean War*, which does an admirable job of covering the story.

But it is not only the availability of an accurate and highly readable history which makes the study of World War II so important to the young man of today who would understand the

Navy. This war was our Navy's greatest challenge; it was the first time all the naval resources which had been built up over more than a century were actually tested.

The Civil War engaged all the power of the nation, but the naval side of that war was relatively minor in relation to the land battle. In the Spanish–American War, the Navy won an easy victory over an opponent not really prepared for naval war in the modern sense. World War I saw us involved too late to feel the brunt of the war at sea. In 1941, however, the Navy found itself matched against a tough and determined opponent, flushed with victory over almost 10 million square miles of land and sea in a series of well-coordinated strikes; an opponent which had trained at sea for years to attain a state of readiness unmatched by any other navy of the time; an opponent which had mastered the new art of carrier war and demonstrated it by opening the conflict with one of the most devastating naval strikes in history.

No modern war can be a one-service affair. The joint effort of the services under a unified commander in a given theater is essential, as the experiences of World War II proved. Still, the very nature of the Pacific war, the vast distances involved, the dependence of Japan upon sea transport, and the shape of Japan's scheme for ultimate hegemony over the entire Asian sea-bordered area, all combine to make the Pacific war of particular interest to the student of naval conflict.

It remains today the primary historical example of modern naval warfare. As such, it deserves our careful study. Such study will not reveal the technological or tactical shape of future conflicts, for we can see that they will be different in many important respects. But for those examples of command, of leadership, of confusion, of determination, of triumph over circumstances which the skillful reader of history always attempts to uncover, the story of the Pacific war has no equal.

To grasp the sweep of the Pacific war in the spring of 1942, try to visualize the map of that vast ocean with Japan's area of conquest running down most of its western boundaries. The Philippines, the Carolines, the Marianas, the Gilberts, the Marshalls, Borneo, Celebes, Java, Singapore, Sumatra, French Indo-

China, Burma, Thailand—all had fallen into Japanese control. The next important target was Australia, and it was over this goal that the first great struggles of the war occurred.

The Japanese had not yet swept the islands north of Australia into their control, and they held only the northern portions of the huge, bird-shaped island of New Guinea. Their control of the Solomon Islands, trailing eastward for some 600 miles like colossal wings of the New Guinea bird, was only tenuous. The Japanese planned to consolidate their hold on the Solomons and sweep eastward around the tail of New Guinea to obtain air bases on its southern coast for the push to Australia.

It was here that the issue was drawn. The Americans, staggering from the blow of Pearl Harbor, had spent the first few months of 1942 getting organized as the Japanese swept southward. But with the Solomons and the attempt to push on to Australia, the great struggle began. In the May, 1942 carrier battle of the Coral Sea—the first of this new type of naval battle which was to play an important part in this war—the U.S. Navy pushed back Japan's attempt to send a force around the New Guinea tail.

Coral Sea was important because it marked the first check of the Japanese in their seemingly invincible march. However, it was soon overshadowed by events of even greater import in mid-Pacific. Only a month after Coral Sea, Admiral Yamamoto, commander in chief of the major Japanese forces, attempted to invade and occupy Midway, westernmost of the Hawaiian chain of islands. The Japanese did not take sufficient care in the coding of their naval messages, and Admiral Nimitz received timely warning of the Japanese plan. However, intelligence, to be useful, must be acted upon; history is full of examples where intelligence of great value has been ignored. Nimitz made no such mistake. As four Japanese carrier veterans of the Pearl Harbor strike approached Midway they were met by planes from the *Yorktown*, *Enterprise*, and *Hornet*.

Pearl Harbor was soon partly avenged; by sundown on June 4, all four carriers were either sunk or floating wrecks. By dawn the next day the carriers were gone, and Yamamoto, realizing that without the carriers he had no chance, was in full retreat for his homeland. The Japanese had fought fiercely and well—*Yorktown* had seen her last battle—but it was a brilliant and dramatic victory for the U.S. Navy. A chapter of American history had been in the hands of the young pilots who dove on the carriers of the Rising Sun that morning of June 4—and they did not fail us.

Midway was the great watershed of the Pacific war. We had desperately needed time to harness our industrial machine, call up and train young men, and repair our damage from Pearl Harbor. Midway gave us this time. Yamamoto had made his bid imaginatively and in time, but the combination of resources of the American team—the intelligence men who intercepted the messages, the coolly efficient Admiral Spruance who directed the battle, and the brave young men who flew the planes—had proven too much for Yamamoto, and his effort turned to disaster for Japan.

After Coral Sea and Midway, the Japanese were slowly but surely pushed back northward toward their home islands. The great initial tilting was over and the war settled to a bitter, island-by-island struggle. The first battle was for Guadalcanal, the island which anchors the eastward sweep of the Solomons. The six months of fighting for this disease-infested jungle outpost was as violent and desperate as any in American history.

From the night of August 8–9, 1942, when one Australian and three American cruisers were sunk in a surprise attack at Savo Island just off Guadalcanal until its successful conclusion the next February, naval battles were an integral part of the Guadalcanal campaign. The roll call of these battles—Eastern Solomons, Santa Cruz, Cape Esperance, Guadalcanal, and Tassafaronga—will sound through the history of the U.S. Navy as long as it exists.

In this six-month period was packed sea fighting of more varied kinds and intensities than in all the previous history of the Navy. Great carrier battles covered thousands of square miles of sunlit ocean; wild cruiser–destroyer battles were conducted within the narrow confines of the Solomons chain during black, tropical nights on velvet-smooth seas; the U.S. Navy learned by bitter experience what damage well-conducted torpedo warfare could wreak, and it perfected its own damage-control procedures in the process. Tactical control procedures were perfected, and the art of controlling gunfire with radar made tremendous strides. Decades of naval development were packed into those six months. The U.S. Navy could never be the same again. Certain illusions of invincibility and grandeur were gone, and in their place was a practical knowledge based on grim experience.

If anyone thinks the United States did not have a worthy opponent in the Pacific, let him ask the men who fought—both at sea and ashore—for Guadalcanal in 1942.

The Japanese fought stubbornly, even after the loss of Guadalcanal, but the tide was ebbing. All through 1943 they strove to hold the Solomons, but with the fall of Rabaul at its western end, the great battle was over. The question now was: which road to Japan?

By June, 1944, Admiral Spruance was demonstrating the answer as he directed the pre-landing bombardment against Saipan and Guam. The Japanese, under Admiral Ozawa, made a thrust against Spruance's invasion fleet, but their carrier planes met a calamitous defeat at the hands of Admiral Marc Mitscher's pilots. The battle is still called "the Marianas turkey-shoot."

Ozawa escaped with the bulk of his ships—but only to meet defeat on another day. The Pacific war was progressing toward its *Götterdämmerung*.

The Japanese conceived a vastly complicated plan to defend the Philippines: its object was no less than destruction of the United States fleet. But the tides of great wars are rarely changed by convulsive death efforts, and the October, 1944 battle for Leyte Gulf was just that for the Japanese war lords.

The Japanese, as they had throughout the war, fought bravely and well. United States sea power was much too strong for them by now, however, and although individual actions of the Leyte Gulf battle were fiercely fought, the victory was an overwhelming one for the Americans.

The Japanese kamikaze planes made the battle for Okinawa a desperately difficult one—over 1900 Japanese suicide planes crashed or attempted to crash into the hulls of our ships around the island—but it was not a naval battle in the true sense of the word.

Fittingly, the Japanese Navy sent out its own version of a kamikaze attack on the sixth of April, 1945, when the super battleship *Yamato* went out to do battle with the U.S. Navy ships at Okinawa. Reportedly, the *Yamato* carried only enough fuel for a one-way trip. On the afternoon of the seventh, Admiral Mitscher's carrier pilots put her beneath the waves and Japanese sea power was effectively finished.

The naval war ended, perhaps symbolically, as it had begun—with the sinking of a battleship.

Throughout the Pacific war the U.S. Navy's submarines fought what was essentially a lone-wolf battle. Only rarely did they participate in the great fleet actions; even more rarely did they come to the attention of the high commanders as they plotted the course of the great campaigns. Still, their contribution was important—about two-thirds of the Japanese merchant ships that went to the bottom were sent there by U.S. submarines. Roughly a third of all the Japanese combat ships sunk in the war were also submarine victims.

Perhaps the best way to convey the flavor of the submarine war is to share some of the experiences I had as a young officer in the submarine *Jack* during the Pacific war. In particular, let's turn our attention to the South China Sea in February of 1944. . . .

The push up the Solomons toward Rabaul was essentially complete and the decision to move next against the Marianas had not yet been taken. This, I know now in the calm perspective of history, was the overall picture. But to those of us engaged in war patrolling (as the submarine missions were called), the overall picture was of limited interest. Our concern was with tankers.

Whatever and wherever the next major move of the war, the Japanese were known to be desperately short of tankers in which to move the petroleum products of the East Indies up to the home islands. The oil was needed to drive their naval ships, but even more serious was the Japanese need for aviation gasoline. The carrier battles of Coral Sea, Midway, Eastern Solomons, and Santa Cruz had all taken a terrible toll of trained Japanese carrier pilots. Pilot training takes large amounts of gasoline—and gasoline was a scarce commodity in the homelands of Japan in February of 1944.

And so, as our sleek, gray-painted submarine patrolled the reaches of the South China Sea between the Philippines and what is now Viet Nam, it looked for tankers—tankers plying the sea route between the oil fields of Borneo and the air fields of Japan.

The South China Sea was solely Japanese territory in February of 1944. Spruance and Halsey had not yet breached the barrier of the Marianas and the Philippines. We were in enemy waters and our safety depended upon our alertness and our ability to submerge. All day long we remained under the surface of the sea, searching for enemy ships as best we could by periscope. Under cover of night, however, we could surface, charge our depleted storage batteries, and begin to sweep the surface of the night ocean with our radar—thus greatly extending the breadth and efficiency of our search. What ships we might find we knew would be enemy—there was no identification problem.

In the early morning hours of February 19, I was in the capsulelike conning tower that was built above the main body of the 300-foot-long *Jack*. Only 20 or so feet in length and perhaps 8 feet in diameter, this cylinder held most of the battle-control equipment of the ship. In addition to the all-important radar, it contained both periscopes, the helm, and, in the after portion, the many-dialled computer that enabled us to take the information from periscope or radar, determine the course and speed of enemy ships, and thus aim our torpedoes to hit.

The conning tower was lighted only with the dim red glow that came from its instruments and their dials; the bridge itself was totally dark. A silent helmsman stood at the forward end of the 20-foot cylinder, listening for any order that might come down to him from the bridge. Farther aft the radar operator hunched over his green, fluorescent screen. All the way aft, I looked at the chart as I prepared to take the officer-of-the-deck watch. I noted our position, measuring the distance and direction to some shoal water which the quartermaster of the watch pointed out to the north.

Smoking was permitted in the conning tower, and the lighted ends of the cigarettes glowed warmly in the darkness as the blue-dungareed men went about their tasks. There was a strange combination of boredom and tension in the air; we were both hunter and hunted and the game was to the death. We all knew this, and yet, men being what they are, we reduced it to simpler and less dramatic terms. We were looking for ships to shoot because when our twenty-four torpedoes were gone, we could head back to our base in Fremantle, Australia—for at least a temporary spell of safety and relaxation before another patrol. We knew we were engaged in a historic struggle; we knew the vital importance of sinking the Japanese tankers; we knew the very real danger we lived in from hour to hour; and yet most of our day-to-day thoughts were more mundane. When would we find the targets? When would we shoot the torpedoes? When would we head for Fremantle?

Above us, on the pitch-dark bridge, the officer of the deck and his four lookouts kept their wordless, cigaretteless vigil. With binoculars glued to their eyes, they scanned water and sky for signs of ships or planes that the radar might miss. Radars had been known to fail; alert lookouts, never. Their only physical comfort came in the form of mugs of steaming black coffee, brought from below by fellow lookouts who were temporarily off watch to rest their eyes. Every fifteen minutes, the silence was broken by a new voice: "Permission to come up and relieve the lookout?"

"Granted," from the officer of the deck. With a sigh of relief, one of the lookouts would turn over his binoculars to the new man and go below for his precious rest. The officers of the deck stayed on for two hours at a time, conscious of their responsibility toward eighty or so shipmates below, conscious of the muffled roar of the diesel engines astern, charging into the storage battery amperes that would be needed during the coming day's long submergence, conscious of the probing fingers of the radar antenna that swept tirelessly overhead.

It was about 0400 and the battery charge was nearly completed; only one of the *Jack*'s four big diesel engines snored softly as it fed the last few amperes into the battery and pushed us along through the smooth, phosphorescent tropical water at a leisurely 5 knots. Sipping hot coffee from one of the *Jack*'s white pottery mugs, I leaned over the radar screen and agreed with Radar Technician Caw that it was empty indeed. Yawning, I turned back again to the chart and studied the patrol line we had set up in hopes of intercepting traffic headed for the straits north of Luzon.

Suddenly, I heard the steady motion of the radar antenna stop as Caw reversed it to look again at a sector where he thought he had seen a telltale indication. I glanced over my shoulder questioningly. The monotonous training resumed. Nothing.

In a few seconds the antenna stopped again, almost as though it sniffed something faintly across the sea air. Caw adjusted the tuning knobs of the radar, looked more closely at his screen, and then whistled a low, slow note. Everyone in the conning tower stiffened, but Caw ignored them as he followed routine and made his report to the officer of the deck.

"Radar contact, bearing 315, range 21,000—looks like several ships together."

Lieutenant Kent Lukingbeal, the officer of the deck, followed his training; he turned the ship up toward the radar contact and slowed.

"Call the captain, station the tracking party, put four engines on the line."

Since both my tracking-party station and battle station were at the torpedo data computer in the after end of the conning tower, I did not have far to go. I stepped over to the machine, turned it on with a twist of the selector switch on its face, and listened to the slowly accelerating whirr of its machinery as it started up. I cranked in the bearing and range supplied by Caw and, setting the enemy ship speed at zero, waited to see which way the bearing would move—the first indication of the direction our targets were heading.

Kent reported from the bridge that he could see nothing on the bearing reported by radar; human eyesight was no match for electronics in this situation.

Alert to the orders from the officer of the deck, the engine rooms were springing to life. I could feel the ship tremble as the big diesels started up under the charge of compressed air which the men on watch there were sending into them. The engines would idle until we determined which way our targets were moving, but they would be ready to drive us at 20 knots in the pursuit.

My data computer began to indicate that our targets were heading northwest, toward the Luzon straits and the Japanese home islands. As I set a first guess at target course and speed into the computer, I was conscious of our skipper, Commander Tommy Dykers, looking over my shoulder at the dials.

Dykers had been our captain since the ship had been built and had made both our first two war patrols with us. He had our complete confidence. A 1927 graduate of the Naval Academy, he had spent most of the intervening years in submarines and had commanded one of the old S-boat submarines in Hawaii before the war. He had a well-deserved reputation as a torpedo sharpshooter. Slender, dark, intent, with a voice that sounded like command, he was a real professional; his touch with the submarine was sure, precise, and effective. He was in his late thirties and at the peak of his proficiency in submarining.

"We're in a little too close, Jim; I'll move out to the south and try to pull ahead of this crowd," he said as he stepped up to the bridge. Although the nerve center of the *Jack* was in the conning tower, the skipper's battle station when we were on the surface remained on the bridge. If emergency should strike, he felt that he could handle it best from that position. We were trained to give him the picture orally with all the detail he needed to conduct the battle.

We could feel the *Jack* begin to come alive as, under the skipper's orders, she swung to the southeast to open the range and parallel the eastward motion of the targets. The ship vibrated as it picked up speed. Soon we were knifing through the dark, smooth sea at a little over 20 knots. The radar kept its sensitive fingers on the unsuspecting ships to the north. There appeared to be eight of them.

Within a short time, Kent Lukingbeal, working at his plotting table, had determined the base course of the convoy; he had some idea of the zigzag plan it was following, and we were ready to go in for the attack.

"Sound the battle stations," said Dykers. An incongruous, musical bong-bong-bong echoed through the ship, almost languidly calling the crew of the *Jack* to its task of destruction. Everyone was up anyway—the word of the radar contact had spread through the ship in seconds—and in a minute or so the control room reported, "Battle stations set below."

We moved in with a sort of looping end-run, designed to move in closer to the convoy and at the same time keep as small a silhouette as possible toward the enemy. The moon was now hanging low behind the convoy, and for the first time the bridge watch could see the ships whose movements we had been studying so intently by radar.

Dykers pressed the button of his bridge intercom and in a sort of stage whisper said one word twice: "Tankers—tankers!"

By now it didn't matter to me; Caw and I were so intent on establishing the enemy course for the critical time of firing the torpedoes that the ships had lost their identity as real objects. They had become a mathematical problem to solve. Plot, computer, and radar worked together to get that course. We knew that a mistake of only 10 or 15 degrees could make the torpedoes miss; we knew Dykers was depending on us to get it right—a chance like this might come only once in the war.

Carefully, Dykers worked the *Jack* under the stern of one of the still-unalerted Japanese escort ships. (Our gray-painted fleet submarines were extraordinarily hard to see on the surface at night. I could well remember, during exercises off Fremantle in Australia, being unable to see one of our submarines only a mile distant in clear moonlight when I knew from radar reports exactly where to look.) We slowed the ship and opened the torpedo-tube doors; the *Jack* was as taut as a bow string, every nerve of every crew member straining. The time was near.

Finally, from the bridge: "Start shooting whenever you can." Wisely, Dykers let us decide the exact moment to shoot. We had the precise information and we could best judge when the solution looked right. We set the bearings and ranges one last time. Everything looked perfect.

"Set!" I called out. "Fire!" said Miles Refo, our executive officer, whose battle station was to supervise the conning tower.

The quartermaster squeezed the firing key just forward of the torpedo computer; the *Jack* lurched faintly as the first torpedo leaped from the bow tubes. Five others followed at six-second intervals—three for each of the two tankers on our side of the convoy. From the bridge, Dykers could see the thin, phosphorescent wakes of the torpedoes stretching out like white strings ahead of the submarine. Surely, the tankers would see them and avoid!

Then a blue flash illuminated the entire water line of the nearest tanker; to those on the bridge it looked close enough to touch. A muffled roar shook the air—then a moment of stillness shattered by a lone, penetrating human scream. Two seconds later the tanker burst into white hot flame from one end to the other. Fire shot hundreds of feet into the air, and the whole area of the sea around the ship became a seething inferno. No one on the tanker could have survived.

Twenty seconds later another blue flash illuminated the convoy as the other tanker was hit. It seemed to those on the bridge as though the entire ocean were lighted up by the flames of the two tankers. Strangely, the Japanese escort ships did not seem to know where we were, or even from which side of the convoy the torpedoes had come. Their guns were firing wildly in the wrong direction, their tracer bullets streaking across the dark sky like great, arching neon signs. We could feel the thump and rumble of depth charges under our feet, and we smiled grimly as we thought of the beating we were avoiding by remaining on the surface.

The diesels gave out a full-throated roar as the *Jack* sped away into the darkness, untouched, and again opened the range to the south as the radar kept its watchful eye on the surviving ships. It soon became apparent that the convoy commander had decided to spend no more time searching for the submarine. He was moving on and taking all his escorts with him.

While the torpedo room forward swiftly reloaded its tubes to be ready to strike again, Dykers weighed the chances of another night attack. The streaks of light in the east showed there simply was not time. The next attack would have to be by day, from periscope depth—an altogether different game.

Dykers informed the crew of his plans over the loudspeaker that went into each compartment of the submarine. Then he secured his people from their battle stations. The tracking party in the conning tower stayed where it was; it would be our task to conn the ship into position for a daytime attack on the remaining three tankers. As we opened the range to the southeast, our plot showed that the Japanese convoy commander had increased the speed of his ships and stopped zigzagging. Apparently he believed he had been attacked by a submerged submarine and was attempting to put as much distance between his convoy and the location of the attack as possible, reasoning correctly that a submerged submarine could not pursue him.

We were, however, not submerged. We sped along on the bright surface of the South China Sea, just over the horizon from the fleeing ships, slowly but surely drawing ahead of them for another attack. We kept them in sight through the long, hot day by means of our periscope, which, raised all the way, gave us a height-of-eye sufficient to see the tops of their masts while they had little or no chance of seeing us.

By late afternoon we had pulled completely ahead of the convoy and had submerged on their apparent track. Here we took a definite chance of losing them. By diving, we lost our height-of-eye and thus lost sight of the convoy. If the commodore had chosen this time to change course radically we might never have seen them again. The waiting period was tense. We realized what a prize this convoy of tankers represented—apparently loaded with already-refined gasoline, judging from the way the ships had gone up the night before—and we were in no mood to lose them now after more than twelve hours of continuous tracking.

Finally, the sonar picked up the sound of echo-ranging and propellers dead ahead—they were coming right down the track! Before long, Dykers sighted them through the periscope. The three tankers were in triangular formation with the three escorts up ahead, echo-ranging steadily as they went. The convoy commander, apparently believing he had left the position of last night's attack far enough behind, had resumed zigzagging.

The atmosphere in the conning tower had changed completely now. The radar was shut down and unattended; the center of attention now was the periscope and the two sonar sets. The red lights were gone and the tiny compartment was lighted in normal white. The almost-casual mood of the night before as the radar tracking went on was replaced by a much more tense quality as the periscope went up from time to time to estimate the range and course of the approaching ships. One thing we knew for certain, now: no matter how successful our attack, we would take a depth-charge beating from the escorts after we had fired our torpedoes. Submerged, our mobility was gone and there would be no more flashing away into the cover of night at 20 knots. We would have to stay quiet and deep—and take it.

Another fact worried us: the sea was so calm it was almost like a mirror. The submariner likes a choppy surface for his attacks so that whitecaps mask the telltale feather of his periscope.

The constant, probing, whine of the Japanese echo-ranging served as a background for our tense conversation. Close down the side of one escort we passed—how could his sonar miss us? How could he miss seeing our periscope in this millpond sea? But on he sped, apparently intent only on searching far ahead; we could hear that his sonar remained set for long-range search.

We were in position to shoot two of the tankers at once. "Final bearing and shoot," snapped Dykers as the periscope slithered up from its well in the deck of the conning tower. Miles Refo carefully set it in the right direction for the skipper to see with a minimum of waste motion. I stood tense by the data computer, ready to put in the new information.

"Check fire—targets have zigged," Dykers said in disgust. He slapped up the folding handles of the periscope—the signal to lower it.

"We can only get one of them now; we'll give him four fish," said the skipper. Time was extremely short; a submarine is in the correct position for a submerged torpedo attack for only a brief moment. If we let them get by, we would be faced with another long period of ending around.

"Final bearing and shoot—up scope," snapped Dykers.

"Mark!" he said as soon as he saw the target tanker.

Miles snapped off the bearings from the periscope scale.

"Set!"

"Fire!"

Three more torpedoes followed at short intervals, all shot with the periscope down. The range was short; there would not be long to wait, one way or another.

Wham! Wham! Wham!

Three hits out of four! The fan of torpedoes we had spread into the ocean had intercepted the side of the speeding tanker just as we had aimed it. Dykers raised the scope and saw another of Japan's precious tankers burning fiercely against the red evening sky in the west.

This time the escorts were not confused; they could see the white lines of torpedo tracks leading to our firing position. Down that line they roared, dropping charges as they came. Our diving officer, Jack O'Brien, took us down as fast as he could.

The movie version of a depth charging is not accurate. They always have the submarine lurching, sailors catching on to pipes for support, lights going out, then magically returning as though someone had slowly turned a rheostat back up. The real thing is at once less dramatic and more disturbing.

The first noise is a sharp metallic crack like a hammer striking a steel plate; a split second later a heavy *bang* like the sound of a large gun going off really thumps the submarine but definitely does not make it lurch or sway—at least not in the experience of submariners who have returned to tell about it. This heavy bang is followed by a several-second-long roar like that of an express train going through a tunnel. If lights are knocked out, they stay out. It is not a pleasant experience—but then neither, I suppose, is being torpedoed with a cargo of oil or gasoline.

After about fifteen minutes of this, during which it began to look as though the escorts were not able to gain sonar contact with us despite their knowledge of our initial location, the convoy commodore apparently once more decided the best plan was to gather up his escorts and make tracks. The depth charging stopped as the sound of the convoy's propellers began to fade into the distance.

We were soon back at periscope depth with nothing in sight. Dykers was not through, however; there were two more tankers and he had fourteen more torpedoes. As the swift-falling tropical night began to settle over the ocean, the dripping, gray-painted shape of the *Jack* emerged from the water and set its bow in the direction of the fleeing ships. The diesels snarled in the still air, and once more the radar reached out with its long fingers to feel the enemy. We had become a surface ship again.

Things had been working too smoothly, however. When the tracking party began to replot the convoy it could find only one ship: a tanker, judging from the size of the radar returns. What had happened? Had the Japanese commodore decided to split his forces? Or had we sunk more ships than we had thought? Stranger things had happened in the quick-changing events of a periscope attack.

We didn't ponder the problem long; submariners are very much of the bird-in-hand school, and we went after the lone tanker with all our attention. It soon became apparent that this lone survivor was going to do all he could to remain one—he was zigzagging wildly. Every two or three minutes he would change course radically. This sort of maneuvering made tracking him a most difficult task. No sooner would Kent Lukingbeal give me one course from the plot than the diverging radar bearings and ranges would make it apparent that he had zigged again.

The tanker was paying for her radical zigs, however, in making a very slow overall progress toward her destination in the Luzon Straits. We found it easy to pull ahead of her and get into firing position. Caw and Kent Lukingbeal worked as a smooth team giving me the new courses, and it wasn't too long before we could tell Dykers that we were holding a pretty good firing solution in the conning tower. Dykers told us to lay down three torpedoes when we were ready.

"Fire!" as the first of the three torpedoes lurched out. Then two more, and we waited with stop watches in hand for the explosions. We looked at each other in disbelief—we had missed!

At the same time, the tanker herself saw us in the gloom. An orange flash illuminated her stern as her deck gun indicated there was fight in our enemy yet. Dykers heard the roar of the shell in the air as it went by the bridge and hit the sea behind us. He swung the big submarine around sharply and it listed heavily as it sped through the flat sea in its turn. The conning tower enunciators snapped to flank speed.

"Maneuvering, bridge, pour it on," said the skipper. No more instructions were required, as word of our situation went back over the battle telephones. Back in the engine rooms, the needles on the dials of the laboring diesels went past the red marks and up against the pegs. Every one of the big engines roared and trembled as it put out the last ounce of power of which it was capable. Our two big bronze propellers churned the ocean as we sped through the darkness.

Another orange flash, and this time the shell landed closer to the bridge; apparently the tanker could see our long white wake trailing astern in the night. But the tanker had picked herself a tough opponent this time; Dykers whipped the *Jack* around quickly and slowed down in hopes that the disappearance of the white wake would make it impossible for the tanker to see us. Apparently the tanker had no useful radar; she had to depend on her lookouts, and our gray camouflage made a tough job for them.

It worked. The tanker's shots continued to follow on our previous track; she had not seen our turn. Once more we pressed in for the attack, this time being careful to hold down the speed and, thus, our wake.

Four more torpedoes sped out in search of the tanker. This time three roaring explosions rent the sky as the brave ship went up in a sheet of white flame. Without a word or a moment's hesitation we pulled away at high speed and commenced a search for the remaining tanker with her escorts. As hours went by with no results we became half convinced that in the attack from periscope depth we might have hit these ships. We had been forced to go deep so quickly we might not have seen all that happened.

In the early morning hours of the twentieth, we broke off the search. Those of us on the tracking stations had been there more than twenty-four hours and now, with the ebbing of excitement, weariness was setting in. We did take time, however, to add up our score: in less than eighteen hours we had fired seventeen torpedoes and sunk four—perhaps five—of Japan's desperately needed tankers.

For a few days all was quiet again with the unchanging cycle of night and day patrol procedures. We did, however, have something to talk about, and the dull hours of every watch were enlivened with stories told and retold of what happened "when we got the tankers."

Then, while patrolling the approaches to Manila Bay, we made contact with an inbound convoy of cargo ships, and before long our remaining seven torpedoes had taken two more of the Empire's ships to the bottom.

Torpedoes gone, we exultantly set our course to the southward. Down through the Sulu Sea, the Celebes Sea, and the Makassar Straits we sped; in the dark of the night we slipped through the narrow passage between Lombok Island and glamorous Bali, then out to the Indian Ocean with Fremantle not far away.

When we arrived, Rear Admiral Ralph Christie, boss of the submarines patrolling from West Australia, had an interesting story to tell us. The commodore of the convoy we had attacked had sent a plain-language message (which had been intercepted) to his headquarters asking for assistance and stating that his convoy was being attacked and destroyed by a wolf pack of at least three American submarines.

Even the news that we had gotten only four of the five tankers couldn't dampen our hilarity at finding ourselves a one-ship wolf pack. We were riding the crest of the wave.

The horror and cruelty of what we were doing did not come home to us; the memory of the smoking ruins of Pearl Harbor were much too strong for that. Sobering events were to come our way, however. Japanese antisubmarine measures in the South China Sea began to improve as the Imperial Navy belatedly realized that the American submarines were eliminating the usefulness of their East Indian oil and rubber resources. Japanese escort ships began to carry radar, and no longer did one submarine sweep the sea of a convoy.

In one month in the summer of 1944, four of our Fremantle-based submarines, including the valiant *Harder*, failed to return from patrol. Close friends were lost and the bitterness of the war increased. Dykers was promoted and retired from war patrolling as younger skippers took over. Miles Refo was given command of his own submarine; other trusted members of our old crew were sent back to the United States to form the nucleus for new ships.

The drivers changed but the submarines stayed on until the end, serving as lifeguard stations for the air strikes on Japan after the sea strength of the Empire had been sapped and there were simply no more ships to hunt.

And so, submarines and destroyers, amphibs and carriers, battleships and PT-boats, cruisers and minesweepers, those who served ashore and those who served at sea, officers and enlisted, uniformed and civilian—all combined to help make the United States Navy in 1945 the greatest sea force in all history.

There were more than 300,000 officers and nearly 3,000,000 enlisted men in the Navy when the war came to a close on the baize-covered table on the quarterdeck of the battleship *Missouri.* Within these vast numbers, the prewar professionals were lost in insignificance, so far as quantity went. But in terms of influence and guidance they had proved to be the mold on which the rest were formed.

Still, the bulk of the strength had come from those who had been civilians on December 7, 1941, and the effort was due as much to their devotion and quality as to the guidance of professionals.

Yet another group of men had made an important contribution. The Allied technologists had made an early and decisively important move when they introduced radar at the very beginning of the war. Neither Germany nor Japan ever realized the full potential of this vital weapon.

Nor did they stop there; greatly improved sonars and target-seeking torpedoes joined with radio transmission direction finders and airborne radar to help defeat the U-boat. Heat-seeking and electronically guided glide bombs opened the way for rockets and missiles controlled the same way. The technologist was moving up in the military hierarchy.

Then, on the morning of August 6, 1945, a bomber incongruously named the *Enola Gay* flew over Hiroshima and toggled out a new type of weapon, and the impact of the scientific revolution on the conduct of war entered a new phase. The scientists, in their attempt to bring the forces of nature to bear on the political enemies of their nation, had introduced a new dimension in the application of force which would give the American military and naval professions the most difficult problems they had faced in their history.

Tradition is important but it must act as a backdrop to our thinking, not a substitute for it. The Navy treasures its traditions, but nuclear weapons and the other problems of the closing decades of the twentieth century point in new directions for which tradition offers small guidance.

Tradition is important to the Navy, and those who close their minds to it, claiming that the scientific revolution has invalidated all the lessons of the past, are shutting off a most valuable source of insight and inspiration. On the other hand, those who claim that nought has changed and that the eternal principles of war have not been affected by the technological developments of the past few decades are closing their minds to the realities of the present.

The scientific revolution is the most significant development of the twentieth century. It is changing our society and the course of world events in profound and far-reaching ways. The truly professional military or naval officer must be alert to both the substance and meaning of this revolution—and the ways in which it dictates changes in the defense of our nation.

CHAPTER EIGHT

What about the Navy's Future?

The demise of the United States Navy has been frequently predicted and, on more occasions than one, solemnly proclaimed. From its birth and throughout most of the nineteenth century, many earnest and sincere Americans believed that the geographical isolation of our nation made any but a coastal defense force unnecessary and, worse, wasteful of Federal funds. One of the most intelligent and gifted men in our history, Thomas Jefferson, held through most of his life that the Navy could consist of a sort of seagoing Minute man force, equipped with small boats mounting only a single gun.

The development of the submarine at the beginning of the twentieth century brought prediction of the end of the fighting ship, and the introduction of the airplane into warfare a few years later gave rise to the same sort of prophecy.

The year 1945 saw three events of enormous historical significance: the defeat of Nazi Germany, the introduction of nuclear weapons, and the defeat of Japan. All were held to foreshadow the decline of the American Navy—for who was left to fight at sea? There simply were no other great navies. What would be the impact of nuclear weapons on sea power? Could not a single nuclear blast eliminate a fleet?

In less than a decade, the Korean conflict had demonstrated the answer to many of these questions. Fought 5600 miles from our mainland, this first important post-Hiroshima struggle was clear evidence of the continuing need of the United States for both sea power and a non-nuclear warfare capability. The appalling logistic demands of the Korean War could not then—or now—be met with air transport. The amphibious landing at Inchon was one of the pivotal events of the conflict. Korea demonstrated that the overseas responsibilities of the United States require the use of the sea whether or not other nations possess warships to contest that use.

The subsequent crises at Lebonan and Quemoy furnished further concrete evidence of the utility of sea power in the present era.

Why is it then, that the future of the Navy is so frequently challenged? Why is it that new technological and political developments are so often accompanied by predictions of decreased importance of sea power? I believe the answer is fairly simple: the use of the sea as a factor in national power is not a self-evident concept. Unlike the use of armies in war, or even of air power, the contribution of the naval forces is often an indirect one—indirect but essential.

History is replete with examples. It was Rome's use of the sea—neither elegant nor professional but adequate—which enabled her finally to prevail over Carthage. Mahan, with his "far distant, storm-beaten ships," immortalized the role of the Royal Navy in containing Napoleon; and Bonaparte himself said, "Had I been master of the sea, I could have been lord of the Orient."

Hitler's generals proved themselves masters of the land war in Europe, but the small sea-barrier of the English Channel was too much for his planners to bring within their grasp. The brilliant use of radar, the bravery of the RAF, the magnificent courage and leadership of Winston Churchill—all of these contributed significantly to the survival of Britain in 1940. But fundamental to the issue was the fact that the Germans simply were not equal to the complex and difficult task of launching a viable seaborne invasion force against England. The Channel was wide for Napoleon, but the technology of modern warfare had made it even wider for Hitler.

History notwithstanding, the importance of sea power is repeatedly overlooked or minimized because of its often indirect nature. Men live upon the land, and it is on this quarter of the earth's surface that the vast majority of today's political and economic activities occur. The sea is a vast desert; many understand its uses and potentials but imperfectly. Ancient as its conquest now is, it remains a realm outside the experience of most of the world's people.

Moreover, an understanding of the role of the sea in warfare requires a more-than-cursory knowledge of war itself: of the importance and difficulty of maintaining a supply line in modern war, with its voracious appetite for heavy equipment and petroleum products; of the difficulty involved in landing a modern army with its equipment upon a hostile beach, or even in projecting it across a hostile strip of ocean. I have known very few experienced Army or Air Force officers who did not have a genuine appreciation of the importance of the Navy, and the reverse is most certainly true. One of the marks of a professional officer is his understanding of the roles played by his sister military services.

History and professional appreciation are still not enough, however, to satisfy those who question the future usefulness of a Navy for the United States. A young man contemplating a career in the Navy is bound to hear such questions—frequently from sources he respects. Such questions cannot help but raise doubts, and in this chapter I shall try to answer them objectively.

The modern nation-state is far from perfect; within the long sweep of history, it may represent only one important step in the evolution of a better political organization. Be that as it may, it is today very much with us, and for better or for worse, it is the framework within which most of us find our self-identification. Most of us are, before anything else, Americans. It is this association which gives us our opportunities, our obligations, and our freedom. One of those obligations in the present world is the maintenance of effective armed forces for the United States.

Accepting this argument, then, at its face value, let us examine the potential usefulness to our nation of the Navy. First, it can protect our own seaborne commercial cargo and deprive an enemy of the use of the seas for cargo shipment. Second, it can launch our own seaborne invasion forces, with the necessary troops and heavy equipment, and prevent an enemy from launching theirs. Third, it can launch our own missile attacks upon land masses, and prevent an enemy from launching missile attacks against us.

Let us talk first about cargo. Each year about 300 million tons of commercial cargo are carried by ship between the United States and Europe—some 100,000 shiploads. The tonnage that goes by air is insignificant in comparison. In fact, about 99 per cent of the world's overseas commerce moves by ship. The reason for this disproportion is simple economics: one gallon of ship's fuel oil moves about 20 times more weight of cargo than a gallon of aviation fuel—and ship's fuel is significantly cheaper. Other costs per ton of cargo carried, such as capital investment, personnel expenses, and maintenance are roughly in the same 20-to-1 category. These are hard and inescapable facts, and the prospects of a significant change in the foreseeable future are small. Where speed is paramount and bulk is small, transoceanic air freight is worth the cost; in other areas the ship will have the center of the stage for a long time to come.

But granted that ships will do most of the trans-ocean cargo carrying, how much is the United States interested in this sort of thing? Isn't our merchant marine shrinking? These questions can best be answered by noting that more than one-third of the entire annual industrial production of the world and about one-half of its annual supply of raw materials are channeled into or out of the United States—the vast majority by ship. Our national merchant marine is indeed shrinking, but for reasons that have nothing to do with our national use of ocean shipping. Each year sees an increase in the total use of such transportation by the United States—and a decrease in the proportion which travels in U.S.-owned and operated ships. Nevertheless, most of this cargo travels in Free World ships—and its protection at sea in the event of war would fall largely to the United States.

Are seaborne invasion forces a thing of the past? Will airlifts replace this previously important function of the Navy? Much argument has swirled about this point since the end of World War II, and there is little doubt as to the growing usefulness of airlifted forces. However, for heavy forces which must remain and fight against opposition, the sheer weight and bulk of equipment required precludes sole reliance on air-landing or parachute-landing techniques. The ability to land across hostile beaches gives its possessor great flexibility in modern warfare. As is the case in many arguments as to military techniques, a combination of capabilities is best. A nation with the strength and commitments of the United States can and must maintain forces which can invade in a variety of ways and against a variety of kinds of opposition. Our present mix of airborne, airlifted, seaborne, and amphibious-capable troops gives us a range of choices which could not be obtained if we relied solely on one technique.

The seas remain an important highway of the world for fighting troops. No overflight or landing rights are required; no political ties are involved in their use. Troops and equipment embarked in ships are flexible in their movement. They can keep the sea for long periods of time, remaining if necessary, just over the horizon in a world trouble spot, ready to move in on short notice if required. When they arrive, they have the heavy equipment and supplies to remain and fight. The partnership of the Navy and the Marine Corps in this highly specialized type of warfare is most important in the complex international struggles of today, in which options and flexibility play so important a role.

Paradoxically, the same modern technology that at first raised so many questions about the continued usefulness of navies has given a new capability to sea forces that seems to be accepted by almost everyone. Few critics of sea power question the usefulness of Polaris, those far-ranging, ever-present nuclear-powered submarines which remain constantly ready to strike far inland with their powerful ballistic missiles. Here the impact of sea power is not indirect, but direct and easily understood. Polaris has given this nation a most important new capability in its effort to protect its independence and freedom. Conversely, the Navy has a new and most important challenge to help develop techniques which will enable the United States to defend against attacks launched in such a manner.

There is, of course, a duality in each of the Navy's missions. It must learn to deny as well as protect the use of the sea in whatever manner is necessary—the sea is neutral and cares not which nation exploits it for the sake of national power or national defense. The struggle, however, is not quite so equal as might at first appear.

Despite the fact that throughout our history there have been intelligent and influential men who questioned the usefulness of sea power, the prevailing opinion within the United States has favored the maintenance of a Navy. Support for the Navy has ebbed and flowed, but never disappeared. Generalizations about nations and national characteristics are dangerous, but by and large the United States has an inherent understanding of the sea, a flair for its uses, and a tradition of expertise in coping with its dangers and enjoying its challenges. Our maritime tradition is strong; our shipbuilders have always been among the world's best; our whalers were as capable and resourceful as any who have ever sailed; our merchant marine has gone through many ups and downs but few have challenged its competence; even our use of the sea for recreation has been marked with competence and skill. Our long-time good performance in the America Cup competition is not only because the races are sailed in U.S. waters.

We are, of course, not the only nation in the world with a great sea tradition and competence, but we are by far the largest modern industrial power so blessed. This combination is not without significance on the world scene. As Alfred Mahan pointed out long ago, modern sea power makes great demands on the industrial power and wealth of a nation. Modern warships—nuclear-powered or otherwise—are crushingly expensive and can only be built and maintained in numbers today by a great industrial nation. It is of no little importance to the Free World that the United States, with its wealth and industrial capacity, is also possessed of a long seagoing heritage.

It is often asked why the superpowers of the Communist world have not made greater use of the sea, why they have no aircraft carriers, no significant amphibious capability. Is it possible that, great land powers that they are, they have not completely understood the potentials of the sea in the modern world? Their recent attempts to build up both their merchant marine and their naval forces may indicate the beginnings of a different view.

Although there is, in objective fact, much reason to predict the continued participation of the Navy in America's armed forces, this does not mean that the naval profession is without problems.

The advent of nuclear weapons, missiles of intercontinental range, and guidance systems of high accuracy have combined to create unprecedented military problems in a world still divided into areas of different political beliefs. The time element, so important in pre-1945 military history, has been almost eliminated. The estimate of the actual capabilities of a potential enemy to inflict damage upon one's homeland has become a different and most dangerous problem.

The challenge to the military profession—whether specialists in land, air, or sea warfare—is a new and serious one. Deciding which weapons systems to develop and in what amounts, how they should be deployed, and how to maintain a spectrum of capabilities from nuclear through limited to guerrilla war in an era of rapidly increasing costs—all of these and a host of other decisions make the military professions of today one of the most challenging in our nation.

To take one example, the military and naval professions have long been concerned with the decision-making process. Over the years they have developed a technique called "estimating the situation" in which, first, the problem is stated clearly and all of the available facts pertinent to its solution are gathered and set down as objectively as possible. Second, the problem is analyzed from each of several specialized viewpoints. Third, while final judgment is suspended, several courses of action which might solve the problem or achieve the objective are formulated. Fourth, these proposed solutions are weighed as to their potential effectiveness against all varieties of circumstances that might influence their execution. Last, taking into consideration the facts, the opinions of the specialists, and the sort of war-gaming that has been applied to the several proposed courses of action, the commander makes his final decision. This is then reduced to writing, and directives implementing the decision are sent out.

Although somewhat ponderous in description, this technique is effective in use. In fact, it is not fundamentally different from the procedures used by any experienced decision-making group, whether the directors of a modern corporation weighing the pros and cons of building a new plant, or just a husband and wife sitting down to see whether the budget will stand the projected cost of a new house.

But is the estimate process competent to cope with the problems of modern defense? In some cases, undoubtedly yes. In others, no. Both the expense of modern defense systems and their importance give such decisions new dimensions which demand more precise techniques if they can be made available. Modern mathematical theory and computer techniques indicate that perhaps they can be. The late John von Neumann's writings on game theory have opened the path for speculation on more precise methods of making decisions in the field of national defense. A new technique known as *systems analysis* is beginning to develop in this area.

Recognizing the absence of opportunities to build up empirical data in nuclear warfare, and indeed in many other fields of modern conflict, systems analysis attempts to project a systematic, quantitative study of what various courses of actions we might choose would accomplish in various situations. An attempt is made to reduce these situations to expressions which can be programmed into digital computers and thus swiftly and thoroughly explored.

The modern manager of national defense—be he civilian or uniformed—is constantly faced with the comparison of alternatives. Arguments can be, and are, made for each set of alternatives—often with eloquence and force. But which is genuinely in the best interests of the nation? Systems analysis offers the decision-maker more than did the old estimate of the situation. It can, if properly handled, make estimates as to the validity of the assumption on which the problem is based, and it can quantitatively compare costs, manpower, and time involved in each alternative. It can even help in formulating new alternatives if those originally projected seem inadequate.

It is most important to keep in mind that the computers themselves can do nothing mysterious or superhuman for us. As one authority in this field often remarks, "the beasts are stupid." But they are fast. Properly programmed, they can explore hundreds of thousands of alternatives very accurately and very quickly. Many of today's complex military problems can be solved only by a seemingly hopeless series of cut-and-try solutions. Hopeless, perhaps, to old methods, but not to a properly programmed computer. This is a new field of learning that faces the military profession squarely in the years ahead. It is replete with esoteric terms such as *linear programming* and *Monte Carlo codes*—but it has real importance and promise, not only in the defense of our nation but in many other fields as well.

The example of systems analysis has been chosen as only one of many fields in which the military and naval professions offer new and fascinating challenges. There are many others. The Navy must, by definition, remain abreast of the newest in technological development. Nuclear-propulsion plants, gas turbines, hydro-jet propulsion, high-performance jet aircraft, better helicopters, improved missiles for antisubmarine warfare, lasers, and the ever-increasing use of digital computers all occupy the modern naval officer in his attempts to keep up with his profession.

The young man attempting to understand the Navy of the future should not be misled into believing that men will be less important as machines and equipment become more complex. Quite the opposite is true. The rugged seagoing man is still of great importance in the Navy, and the need for officers and enlisted men armed with sophisticated knowledge is growing every day. Inevitably, as both the ships and the society change, our enlisted men are also changing. Always dependable, always competent, the new enlisted man retains these fine characteristics of his predecessors but, in addition, brings to the Navy an increasing amount of expertise and knowledge. He is, inevitably, more demanding of his leadership, and never has the challenge to our officers been so great in this area as today. The educational difference between officer and petty officer may be much smaller than it once was, and as a result, both parties to the relationship must bring to bear great understanding and dedicated performance. High moral character, mental alertness, tolerance, and a broad understanding of our nation's position and problems are increasingly characteristic of our enlisted personnel. Working with these young Americans in a leadership position represents an extraordinary challenge in itself.

The naval profession has many dimensions, and they cannot be mastered all at one time. First things must come first, and a fundamental knowledge of the sea and ships must precede all else. I think it can be said, however, that any young man embarking on a naval officer's career today can rest assured of two fundamental points: the Navy will be around in force for some time to come, and there will be plenty of challenge for his energies, no matter how great they are.

CHAPTER NINE

After All, Is It Worth It?

As I observed at the outset of this book, the choice of a career may be influenced by many factors. Each young person must, in the long course, make this choice for himself. What may bring great rewards and happiness to one will be ashes in the mouth of another. Each of us has his own ideals and his own concept of what life should be. Still, with all the variations in our outlooks, there are elements of similarity. There are certain aspects of the naval profession which interest us all and which may shed some light on the problem for everyone.

There is, first of all, the long view. Each of us has, at best, about forty years of really active, productive time in which we must accomplish most of what we hope to do within our lifetime. Our society dictates with increasing emphasis that each young person spend the first twenty to twenty-five years of his life in a learning environment before he can participate in the management or professional affairs of the community; in many cases the time span is approaching thirty years. Despite a few outstanding exceptions, most of us have passed the time of useful contribution by the time we reach the age of sixty-five or seventy.

Although the perspective of youth is such that these ages seem eons away, the truth of the matter is that time is short and the course is run almost before one knows it has begun. What is really of importance? What can one do with these few precious years that will, in retrospect, seem worthwhile? We pass a cemetery and see endless acres of markers. We reflect upon the fact that each of these now-gone persons' lives was, to them, as exciting and important as ours are now to us. And yet who can remember who they were, what they did, their hopes, their fears, their frustrations? Even their names?

In searching for the longer values in our lives, in looking for what might be of permanent value, we come back inevitably to the concept of service. To spend one's small span of time in self-seeking pursuits alone would be hollow and fruitless to most of us. The concept of service to others or to an institution of value has a permanent ring in a time of increasingly transient values. It is, as we have seen, a basic ideal of most of the professions. The goal of useful service to others is strong in medicine, law, teaching, and the ministry.

The attraction of service to one's country will inevitably depend upon one's view of his native land. It is admittedly an intensely personal matter. But each of us must think it through—it is one of the most fundamental of our values. Without hypocrisy or uncertainty I can say that, in my view, useful service to America is one of the most powerful and effective forces upon this planet for freedom and for what most men call good.

Doubtless, there are many other nations of just as much intrinsic worth, whose ideals are just as high, whose heritage is just as proud. But none of them, to my knowledge, can match our size, or power, or wealth. In short, the United States represents an enormous potential for *effective* good in a world which faces an era of unprecedented crisis in the decades ahead. There is every indication that the world approaches difficulties it has not known before: the population explosion, the paradox of rich nations growing richer and poor nations poorer—these and many other problems indicate that the world is approaching a new period in its history. There are several rays of hope, however, and the wealth, power, and good will of the United States is one of the brightest. Is there any better ideal than to serve it in that area where we think we can make our own best contribution?

To some, such long-term philosophical thoughts may be of value, to others, not much. To all of us, however idealistic, there are other considerations. It is difficult indeed to sustain one's attachment to an occupation on the thin air of ideals alone. Most of us want other, more tangible, values in our work.

Let me point out one aspect of the naval profession that escapes the attention of many young people—many, in fact, who are already naval officers. This is the matter of variety. No matter what our devotion to a given field of work, it must provide a certain amount of variety to retain its interest. In many professions, the variety comes from the people with whom one deals. The doctor, the lawyer, the teacher—each finds variety and challenge in the different problems and conflicts of his clients or pupils. Nevertheless, each of these professions can, on occasion, find a certain sameness in overall pattern from year to year.

The naval officer may spend two or three years in a ship, then two years teaching, then two years on a staff dealing with administrative matters, then find himself back in another ship, but this time in command. The first duty may be on a ship based in California, the teaching at Annapolis, the staff duty in London, and the command in a ship based in Florida. Occupationally and geographically, the naval officer finds variety. Some people love it, others find it a hardship. Most, in the long run, find that it keeps their outlook broad and their interest high. Running through it all, giving it a pattern of unity, are all the threads of the naval profession; but variety is part and parcel of the naval officer's life, and a young man contemplating it would do well to ask himself (and his wife, if he has one) about this aspect of the Navy. Wives are particularly important in evaluating this part of the Navy life. I have known very few men who, strictly for themselves, did not genuinely enjoy these frequent changes. I have known several whose wives disliked moving so much that, in the long run, the Navy became unsuitable for their husbands.

There is another facet of the naval profession that often escapes the attention of outside observers or newcomers: fellowship. This may sound a bit quaint to today's generation, but let me explain what I mean. A ship at sea is a community apart, and its wardroom can become the source of long friendships that, elsewhere, in the distractions of modern life, might not have time to be formed. Each profession has its fair share of attractive and unattractive members. There is, however, in the absence of competition and scramble in the Navy an opportunity for companionship which, I believe, escapes other walks of life today—perhaps even the other services. There remains something about the isolation of a ship during long periods of time at sea which has found no exact counterpart elsewhere in our modern world.

The sound friendships of Navy life are, thank goodness, not restricted to shipboard life. Navy families, quite understandably, become good friends during tours of duty. They often renew those friendships in new places, strange to both families. The difficulty of moving within the Navy is considerably softened by the knowledge that at the new station there will be old friends whom one has not seen for years. Each new move is not a move to a strange town but, increasingly as one's circle of friends widens, a move to an area where many, many old friends are found. Their hospitality and their willingness to help during the period of getting settled are among the Navy's oldest, and most pleasant, traditions.

Getting back to the man's point of view, another of the experiences the Navy offers which is unique, in my view, is that of command at sea. There are few experiences left in the modern world more satisfying, more challenging, more rewarding, and, to most men, more downright fun than having command of a ship at sea. There are times of heartache and regret, times of frustration and fury, and not a few of just plain hard work, but when it is all over, it is one of the really grand experiences of one's life.

Leaving aside the personal satisfactions of command, there are some longer-term rewards. Successful ship command almost always leaves a man different for having had it. To those who have not witnessed the change in others, the statement probably sounds pompous and conceited. But again and again, I have seen young men I have known for a long time take their first command and with it responsibilities and authority they have not known before. In the two or three years that they hold that command, if they hold it successfully—and the great majority do—a definite change in self-confidence, decisiveness, and self-reliance comes about. For those who may think the effects of command at sea are all on the overbearing side, let me hasten to add that if there is a single man who has not learned humility during his tour of command, then he has either escaped the usual experiences or he is impervious to such instruction.

In short, command at sea is a great teacher, and fortunate is the man who stays with the naval profession long enough to go through this course of instruction. He will benefit from it all his life, regardless of what he may later do.

There is, then, the matter of advancement. Each of us likes to have the feeling that he is progressing, that the passing years are adding something beside extra pounds and graying hair. In many a life's work there comes a day, often much too early, when one finds that the road to further advancement has been permanently blocked. Somehow, for some reason, there will be no further reward, no higher recognition.

This must happen, inevitably, to everyone someday—but its timing is all-important. At a late enough date and at a high enough level, it is welcome to all but an insatiable few. The Navy has been wise in the construction of a promotion system which offers a continuing prospect of advancement over a long period of time for many of its officers. Each officer who applies himself with vigor, has a goodly supply of competence, and enjoys reasonably good luck (as Admiral Nelson observed, some of it is essential to a naval officer), has a good chance of selection for each of the grades on the naval ladder through captain. This is not to say that it is a certainty. For several years now, the annual selection to the rank of captain has taken fewer than half of those in the zone. Those who are looking for security and assured promotion should not look to the Navy. But for those who like the challenge of competition, who like the concept of recognized promotional steps from time to time throughout one's active service, the Navy has much to offer.

But all of these factors—service, variety, friendship, command at sea, competition for advancement—all of these are as nothing unless you, yourself, are persuaded that the game is worth the candle.

There is no profession, no calling, in the world worth its salt that does not have its frustrations and sacrifices. There is almost no profession whose members do not feel that, somehow, the world at large does not truly appreciate the value and worth of its contribution. Even those most prestigious of modern professions, medicine and law, have their gnawing doubts, and their members express, both in conversation and in print, anxiety over the declining public image of their calling and the failing of those ideals which once illuminated their paths. Moral: think twice before allowing self-doubts expressed by naval officers themselves to undermine your determination. Such doubts are not restricted to the naval profession, and in any event the decision must be yours alone.

To paint the naval profession as a bed of roses would be to insult the reader's intelligence; if, indeed, the profession were anything of the sort, it would not be worthy of long consideration. It is tension, conflict, and the possibility of disappointment that create the environment for a sense of achievement and reward. Those who seek great material rewards obviously should look elsewhere, but to those who can find satisfaction in a life of useful service, filled with challenge, offering opportunities for real adventure and many, many enriching experiences, it may prove the best of all possible choices.

One thing must be remembered; it is not just a job, it is a way of life. One must be caught up in it bone and marrow to find its deepest rewards. In today's Navy, significantly different from that of the pre–World War II era, few new officers are full-blown, predetermined professionals. The training, the experience, the education (much of it self-administered), the refinement by fire, and the continuing competition and selection work their effects through the years until, at some time not easily defined or identified, a true professional is created. Once this has happened, a change has occurred which will not easily pass.

Most of the elements of this essentially practical profession are open and plain for all to see. It has aspects, however, like all professions worthy of the name, that go deeper; there is an indefinable dimension, a sort of mystique, that does not yield its secrets to the casual inquirer or, indeed, to many who wear the Navy's blue and gold for many years. Its deepest characteristics are as inscrutable as that combination of the sea and service to country that gives the profession its distinctive flavor.

Is it worth it? Every man must speak for himself. As for me, the answer is yes. It has been worth it, over and over again.

Appendix A

Although the detailed regulations may change from year to year, there are certain facts which a young man interested in attending the Naval Academy—and his parents—should understand from the outset. The following excerpts from the Naval Academy Admissions Regulations for 1965 are reprinted as an aid in this direction.

104. Engagement to Serve (10 U.S.C. 6959)

Each midshipman who is a citizen or national of the United States shall sign an agreement that, unless sooner separated, he will:

(1) complete the course of instruction at the Naval Academy;
(2) accept an appointment and serve as a commissioned officer of the Regular Navy or the Regular Marine Corps for at least five years immediately after graduation; and
(3) accept an appointment as a commissioned officer in the reserve component of the Navy or the Marine Corps, and remain therein until the sixth anniversary of his graduation, if an appointment in the regular component of that armed force is not tendered to him, or if he is permitted to resign as a commissioned officer of that component before that sixth anniversary.

If the midshipman is a minor and has parents or a guardian, he may sign the agreement only with the consent of the parents or guardian.

Officers of the Armed Services serve at the pleasure of the President, and no terminal dates are established for their commissions.

105. Entrance Date

The fourth class summer program is of nine weeks duration beginning the ninth Tuesday preceding Labor Day. The Academic year begins on the first Wednesday following Labor Day. Each eligible candidate will be notified individually by the Bureau of Naval Personnel of the hour and date he is to report to the Naval Academy for admission.

Part II. Nominations

201. General

It is necessary for a young man to obtain a nomination in order to be considered for appointment to the Naval Academy. The sources of nominations are described below and the applicant should study carefully the various sources to determine those through which he is eligible to apply. College Board test results taken for purposes of qualifying for the Naval Academy apply to all nominations a candidate may hold.

202. Types of Nominations

202.1 Congressional

Each Senator, each Representative, and the Resident Commissioner of Puerto Rico individually may have a maximum of five midshipmen attending the Naval Academy at any one time. The applicant should address his request directly to the official concerned. Eligibility for Congressional nominations is restricted by law to the two Senators from an individual's home state and to the Representative of the Congressional district in which he lives. A sample letter of application is included below.

202.2 Vice Presidential

The Vice President may have a maximum of five midshipmen attending the Naval Academy at any one time. He may nominate candidates from the United States at large. A letter requesting nomination should be addressed directly to the Vice President. It should contain the same information required of a Congressional applicant.

202.3 District of Columbia

The Commissioners of the District of Columbia may have a maximum of five midshipmen attending the Naval Academy at any one time. Applications should be made directly to the Commissioners of the District. A letter requesting nomination from the Commissioners should contain the same information required of a Congressional applicant.

202.4 Governors of Puerto Rico, The Canal Zone, the Virgin Islands, Guam and American Samoa

The Governors of Puerto Rico and the Canal Zone each may have one midshipman attending the Naval Academy at any one time. The Governors of the Virgin Islands, Guam, and American Samoa may collectively have one midshipman attending the Naval Academy at any one time. Applications to these nominating authorities should contain the same information required of Congressional applicants.

202.5 Presidential

The President may appoint seventy-five midshipmen each year. These appointments are limited by law to the sons and adopted sons of officers and enlisted personnel of the Regular Army, Navy, Air Force, Marine Corps, and Coast Guard on active duty, retired, or deceased, but not discharged before retirement or death. Adopted sons to be eligible must have been adopted prior to their fifteenth birthday. The Secretary of the Navy is authorized to approve waivers of this policy where adoption proceedings had been initiated but the adoption had not occurred prior to the fifteenth birthday through circumstances beyond the control of the foster parents. Stepsons are not eligible. Applications should be addressed to the Chief of Naval Personnel, Navy Department, Washington, D.C. 20370. Use application form given below.

202.6 Regular Navy and Marine Corps

The Secretary of the Navy may appoint each year eighty-five enlisted men of the Regular Navy and Marine Corps. These men must meet all requirements including the age limitations. In addition they must have enlisted in the Navy or Marine Corps on or before July 1 of the year preceding the desired date of entrance to the Naval Academy. Enlisted men who can fulfill the age and service requirements should make known to their commanding officers early in their enlistment their desire to go to the Naval Academy.

For further information about enlisting in the Navy or Marine Corps, apply to your nearest Navy or Marine Corps Recruiting Station.

202.7 Naval Reserve and Marine Corps Reserve

The Secretary of the Navy may appoint each year eighty-five enlisted men of the Naval Reserve and Marine Corps Reserve. These men must be qualified as to age and must have served in the Reserve for at least one year on 1 July of the year of entrance to the Naval Academy. In addition to all other normal requirements for appointment, these men must be on active duty, or must be members of a drilling unit of the Reserve, be recommended by their commanding officers, and have maintained efficiency in drill attendance with their Reserve Units.

Midshipmen USNR of the Regular NROTC Program and members of the Aviation Cadet Program are not eligible for appointment under this quota.

For further information about enlistment in the Naval Reserve or Marine Corps Reserve, apply to your nearest Navy or Marine Corps Recruiting Station.

202.8 Sons of Deceased Veterans

The President may have a maximum of forty midshipmen, who are the sons of deceased veterans, attending the Naval Academy at any one time.

Eligibility for nomination under this quota is confined to sons of members of the Armed Forces of the United States who were killed in action or have died of wounds or injuries received, or disease contracted, or pre-existing injury or disease aggravated, in active service during (1) World War I or World War II (as each is defined by laws providing service-connected compensation or pension benefits for veterans of World War I or World War II and their dependents); or (2) the Korean conflict beginning 27 June 1950 and ending 31 January 1955. The determination in each case of the Veterans' Administration as to the service connection of the cause of death is binding upon the Secretary of the Navy. Use application form given below.

202.9 Honor Naval and Military Schools

The Secretary of the Navy may appoint annually ten honor graduates of educational institutions designated as "honor schools" by the Department of the Army, Navy, and Air Force. Candidates under the quota will be nominated each year by the heads of the schools designated as "honor schools." Each such school may nominate three honor graduates to compete for the appointments. Included in the three may be students whose standing is such that it appears they will be honor graduates in June of the year in which the examination will be held. However, the latter will not be considered for appointment unless they do fulfill the requirements which would entitle them to be honor graduates at the time of their graduation. Eligible students should apply to the heads of their schools for nomination.

202.10 Naval Reserve Officers' Training Corps (Contract Students Only)

The Secretary of the Navy may appoint annually ten midshipmen from among members of the Naval Reserve Officers' Training Corps. Three candidates may be nominated each year by the president of each educational institution in which an NROTC unit is established. Each candidate must be a regularly enrolled contract student in the NROTC and must have completed one year of scholastic work in the corps at the time of entrance to the Naval Academy. Students should apply to the commanding officers of their NROTC units to request a nomination.

202.11 Sons of Medal of Honor Winners

The son of any person who has been awarded the Medal of Honor for acts performed while in the armed forces may be appointed provided he is in all respects qualified. No recommendation or endorsement from any source is required. Applications for appointment under this paragraph should be addressed to the Chief of Naval Personnel, Navy Department, Washington, D.C. 20370.

203. Qualified Alternates and Competitors

203.1 General

The Secretary of the Navy is authorized, upon recommendation of the Academic Board of the Naval Academy, to appoint 150 qualified Congressional alternates. Additional appointments from qualified alternates and competitors may be made by the Secretary of the Navy to bring the Brigade of Midshipmen to its authorized strength. If additional appointments are possible after the 150 qualified Congressional alternates have been appointed, at least 75 per cent of these additional appointments must be selected from Congressional nominees and not more than 25 per cent may be made from non-Congressional sources. All qualified alternate and competitive candidates will be considered and no special application by the individual is necessary or desired.

204. Foreign Students

204.1 Republic of the Philippines

The Secretary of the Navy is authorized to permit, for the President of the United States, not exceeding four Filipinos at a time to receive instruction at the United States Naval Academy. Applications for appointment from this source must be addressed through diplomatic channels of the Government of the Republic of the Philippines. The appointments are on a competitive basis.

204.2 American Republics other than the United States

The Secretary of the Navy is authorized to permit, upon designation of the President of the United States, not exceeding twenty persons at a time from the American Republics other than the United States to receive instruction at the United States Naval Academy. Not more than three persons from any one of such Republics shall receive instruction at the same time. Applications for these appointments must be addressed through the appropriate diplomatic channels of the applicant's country. The appointments are on a competitive basis.

205. Nominating Methods

205.1 Congressional

A member of Congress may choose between two methods of nomination as follows:

(1) Principal-Alternate Method

He may nominate one principal candidate and five alternate candidates listed in order of his preference. If the principal candidate meets the eligibility criteria and qualifies on the entrance examination, he will be offered the appointment. If the principal does not meet the minimum requirements, the next designated alternate candidate who qualifies will be chosen.

(2) Competitive Method

He may nominate six candidates and authorize the Naval Academy to select his best qualified candidate. A selection score will be determined for each qualified candidate. It will include all entrance examination scores, ratings on previous academic achievement and extra-curricular activities, and a rating based primarily upon the recommendations of school principals and teachers. The candidate having the highest score will be offered the appointment.

205.2 Other Categories

The choice between the principal-alternate and competitive methods is also available to the Governors of Puerto Rico and the Canal Zone. The Governors of the Virgin Islands, Guam, and American Samoa may nominate only on a competitive basis for the one appointment allowed.

Candidates will be selected for appointment on a competitive basis from nominees entered in the several service-connected categories: Presidential, Sons of Deceased Veterans, Regular and Reserve Components, Honor Military and Naval Schools, and NROTC. Factors considered in the competition are all entrance examination scores, previous academic achievement, extracurricular activities and recommendations of school principals and teachers. There is no limit on the number of eligible candidates who may compete in the Presidential, Sons of Deceased Veterans or Regular and Reserve categories. Each honor military and naval school and the President of each institution in which an NROTC unit is established may name three candidates.

The Son of a Medal of Honor winner will be nominated upon application to the Bureau of Naval Personnel. He will be offered an appointment provided he qualifies on the entrance requirements.

205.3 Nominating Schedule

A young man who wants to enter the Academy upon graduation from high school must apply for nomination well in advance of admission. If seeking a Congressional nomination, it is particularly important to apply early, preferably during the spring of the junior year in high school. Senators and Representatives may submit the names of their nominees any time between 1 July and 31 January for the class entering in June. A majority of them will make their selections for nomination early in this period. A young man who waits until the fall or winter months to apply cannot be considered if the Member of Congress has already selected his quota of nominees.

Other nominating authorities must also submit their nominations between 1 July and 31 January.

206. Civil Service Commission Examinations for Congressional Nominations

It is the policy of some of the authorized nominators to have the U.S. Civil Service Commission hold special competitive examinations solely for the purpose of assisting them in selecting their candidates. These special competitive examinations do not determine the candidate's scholastic qualifications for admission to the Naval Academy. The Naval Academy requirements must still be met fully. All the details concerning administration of the special competitive examinations are handled by the nominator concerned and the U.S. Civil Service Commission in Washington. Correspondence in regard to these examinations should be addressed to the Member of Congress.

Part III. Qualifications for admission

Summary of Changes Effective with the Class Entering in June 1965

Significant changes, all discussed in detail in appropriate portions of this Appendix, are as follows:

1. The development of new Mathematics Achievement Tests by the College Entrance Examination Board.
2. The inclusion of class standing in high school as a qualifying factor.
3. The consideration of previous college records as a qualifying factor.
4. The requirement that all candidates take the College Board Test.
5. The requirement that a candidate qualify in the year in which he is seeking admission.
6. Revised medical examination procedures which permit examination of candidates at Navy, Army or Air Force facilities.

301. General Requirements

All candidates must meet certain general requirements of citizenship, age, marital status, and moral character.

301.1 Citizenship
All candidates must be citizens of the United States except as specified in Articles 204–206 above.

301.2 Age

Candidates must be at least 17 and not have passed their twenty-second birthday on 1 July of the year of admission.

301.3 Marriage

Candidates must never have been married. Any midshipman who marries will be discharged from the Academy.

301.4 Moral Character

They must be of good moral character.

302. Scholastic Requirements

A candidate's previous academic record and his performance on specified College Entrance Examination Board Tests are the factors which are used to determine scholastic qualification for admission.

There are two methods of qualifying scholastically for admission to the Naval Academy: the Examination Method and the College Certificate Method. These two methods are described in paragraphs 302.3 and 302.4 below.

302.1 Submission of Scholastic Records

Each candidate is responsible for the submission of detailed records of all of his completed high school, preparatory school, and college work and lists of any current or proposed courses. Official forms for this purpose will be provided by the Navy Department following receipt of the nomination from the Member of Congress or other authorized appointment sources. These certificates should be filled out and submitted to the Naval Academy by the school or schools as soon as practicable after receipt. It is important to each candidate that records be supplied promptly and that previous school records include academic marks, class standing or estimated class standing for the first semester of the final year. In the event that class standing for the end of the junior year is the latest available, it will be acceptable. Recommendations from the candidate's high school principal, teachers, extracurricular advisors and coaches should be furnished on the forms provided. These records and recommendations will be considered in conjunction with the test results in order to establish the priority of qualified candidates in the various competitive lists and for the purpose of selection under the qualified alternate law, and must be received not later than 15 March.

It must be appreciated that except for Congressional principals and sons of Medal of Honor holders, it is necessary to take those candidates who have succeeded in qualifying scholastically, medically and in physical aptitude and arrange them in an order of precedence. In assigning a selection score for this purpose to such a qualified candidate, his scholastic record, including College Board scores, rank in high school, extracurricular record, and recommendations are taken into account. Once a candidate is assigned an order of selection score, it remains unchanged in order that it may be used to determine his relative position on any competitive list for which he is eligible.

302.2 Acceptable Secondary School Certificate

An acceptable secondary school certificate is one from an accredited secondary school, or its equivalent, presenting at least fifteen units of credit in college preparatory subjects and indicating ability to do college-level work successfully. While not an absolute requirement, standing in the top 40 per cent of one's high school class is of importance in determining qualification for admission, and the great majority of midshipmen come from the top 20 per cent of their high school classes. Candidates should, insofar as is practicable, include as many as possible of the following studies in their secondary school programs:

a. At least three years but preferably four years of mathematics, including the elements of advanced algebra, geometry and trigonometry.
b. Four years of English.
c. Two years of a foreign language, preferably modern.
d. One year of chemistry.
e. One year of physics.

It is expected that the secondary school official will recommend only those candidates who, in his opinion, have the scholastic background needed to pursue successfully a difficult course of college level in which the emphasis is placed on engineering subjects, as well as the humanities, and who have those qualities of character necessary for success in an institution where training for effective military leadership is of paramount importance.

Deficiencies in the secondary school certificate can often be offset by offering acceptable college work in the subject or subjects involved or advanced related branches thereof. Conversely, evidence of inability to do acceptable college work can be cause for disqualification.

302.3 Examination Method

The basic method of qualifying is by presenting an acceptable secondary school certificate and by scoring acceptably in the scholastic entrance examination consisting of the December, January, or March administrations of the following tests of the College Entrance Board: The Scholastic Aptitude Test (Verbal and Mathematics sections), the English Composition Test, and either the Level I (Standard) or Level II (Intensive) Mathematics Achievement Test. It is the candidate's responsibility to ensure that he takes these required tests. No substitutes will be considered in qualifying for entrance to the U.S. Naval Academy.

In the past, basic qualifying scores have been 500 for the verbal score and 550 for the mathematics score of the Scholastic Aptitude Test, 500 for the English Achievement Test and 550 for the Mathematics Achievement Test. Variations in basic qualifying scores can be expected each year. These tests must be taken during the school year preceding admission. Candidates are encouraged to choose the mathematics achievement test in which they feel they can attain the higher score. Level I is recommended for candidates without advanced high school mathematics. No additional weight is given to the results of the test in Level II Mathematics over those in Level I Mathematics.

Basic qualifying scores in the College Entrance Examination Board Tests for any class will be determined by the Academic Board of the Naval Academy. No candidate shall be admitted to the Naval Academy unless in the opinion of the Academic Board he shows the requisite scholastic qualifications.

Each candidate is responsible for registering with the College Entrance Examination Board for the tests as promptly as possible after receiving the necessary instructions from the Bureau of Naval Personnel, Navy Department, Washington, D.C. These instructions will include the provision for payment by the Navy for these tests. Although the Navy Department will pay for only one administration of the tests, the Naval Academy will accept scores from the other applicable administrations and will credit a candidate with the highest scores achieved.

General information on the tests, including dates of administration, location of testing center, dates by which candidates must register, method of application, etc., is published in a booklet entitled Bulletin of Information. This booklet, published annually by the College Board, may be obtained without charge by writing to either:

The College Entrance Examination
Board
Post Office Box 592
Princeton, New Jersey, 08540
or
The College Entrance Examination
Board
Box 1025
Berkeley, California, 94701

In addition to the above-mentioned Bulletin, the College Board publishes two booklets, one entitled "A Description of the College Board Scholastic Aptitude Test" and one titled "A Description of the College Board Achievement Tests." Supplies of these two booklets are provided by the College Board to all high schools. Candidates can obtain the booklets from their high schools or may write to the College Board for individual copies free of charge.

For the majority of candidates, the examining points are in the communities in which they live. It is expected that few, if any, candidates will have to travel more than seventy-five miles.

Duly nominated candidates who have registered for and are

unable to take the December, January, or March administrations because of sickness, injury, weather, or other extenuating circumstances should promptly advise the Chief of Naval Personnel.

302.4 College Certificate Method

A candidate who holds a nomination as a Congressional principal or alternate or who is seeking admission as the son of a Medal of Honor winner may fulfill the scholastic requirements for admission by submitting an acceptable secondary school certificate and an acceptable college certificate. He is required to take the College Board tests specified in Article 302.3 above for the information of the Naval Academy.

An acceptable secondary school certificate is as described in paragraph 302.2 above.

An acceptable college certificate is one attesting at least one year's attendance at an accredited junior college, college, university or technical institution of college grade during which the candidate completed courses totalling at least twenty-four semester hours of credit for subjects acceptable to the Naval Academy with grades substantially better than the college minimum passing grade. Six semester hours must be in pure mathematics, such as college algebra, trigonometry, analytical geometry, calculus, etc., and six semester hours must be in English or history or a combination thereof. The remaining credits necessary to complete the certificate may be offered from a wide range of college liberal arts or engineering subjects.

The length of college attendance prescribed is defined as requiring actual full-time attendance for one regular school year during which the candidate pursues courses constituting a normal year's load.

A candidate who contemplates qualifying by the College Certificate Method but who has not completed the required year of college at the time of receipt of his nomination should have his high school record and a preliminary college record submitted showing the courses contemplated or in progress and the amount of credit in semester hours to be assigned for each course. Forms for this purpose will be provided by the Navy Department. An early review of the record of completed work and of courses proposed for completion may reveal defects which can be corrected by slight changes in the final semester schedule. The certificate action reports issued by the Naval Academy indicate steps which the candidates should take. However, if in doubt, a candidate should address a letter to the Dean of Admissions, U.S. Naval Academy, Annapolis, Maryland.

302.5 Qualifying in Previous Year

Former midshipmen who have completed successfully the first year of the Naval Academy's course need not requalify scholastically for admission. No other former candidates are exempted from requalifying for the class to which they seek admission.

303. Medical and Physical Requirements

303.1 General

All candidates are encouraged to undergo thorough medical and dental examination by a private physician before pursuing nomination and before taking the qualifying medical examination. This will serve to identify obviously disqualified applicants or those who may have remediable defects which must be corrected at the candidates' expense. Official standards of medical fitness are found in Chapter 15 of the Manual of The Medical Department, U.S. Navy. The candidates who are obviously disqualified will benefit themselves and the U.S. Government by not pursuing candidacies further. All candidates are advised to carry sun glasses for use after eye examination.

303.2 Medical and Physical Aptitude Examinations

The Naval Academy Qualifying Medical Examination determines a candidate's medical status for admission to the Academy. Members of Congress may authorize a Naval Academy Medical Examination, at the authorized Medical Examining facilities, for an applicant to determine his medical qualification. This examination will be considered a final Naval Academy Qualifying Medical Examination. Thus, it will not be necessary for a formally nominated candidate to return to a medical examining facility for further medical examination. Candidates who have a Qualifying Medical Examination on file taken since 1 July 1964 will be required to take only the Physical Aptitude Examination. Formally nominated candidates to the Naval Academy are required to satisfactorily complete a Physical Aptitude Examination which is in conjunction with the Qualifying Medical Examination. This examination includes a series of exercises designed to determine coordination, strength and endurance of the body musculature. Included are sit-ups, pull-ups, arm hang, and a squat walk exercise. It also includes a battery of tests which will bring out disqualifying orthopedic defects such as shoulder, knee, or other malfunctions. Failure to pass any part of this examination will be cause for rejection.

When reporting for Medical and Physical Aptitude Examination, candidates are required to have suitable shorts and supporter for use when undergoing the Physical Aptitude Examination.

Candidates who are ordered to report for Medical and Physical Aptitude Examination and who are unable to take the Physical Aptitude Examination will be required to produce sufficient evidence as to preclude them from such at that time. Insufficient evidence will be cause for their disqualification. Formally nominated candidates who are injured or ill for any reason and unable to comply with instructions to report for Medical and Physical Aptitude Examination are required to communicate with the Chief of Naval Personnel and the scheduled examining facilities to explain the circumstances of the injury or illness before further examination or delay in examination will be authorized. Candidates who have undergone major surgery involving knee, ankle, shoulder, elbow, wrist or spine will NOT be scheduled for examination until six months have elapsed following surgery. Medical and Physical Aptitude Examinations terminate on 15 March. Injury and surgical cases will not be considered after this date. Candidates having orthodontic appliances in place will be required to have them removed prior to reporting for Qualifying Medical Examination.

While candidates may be scheduled for Medical and Physical Aptitude Examinations at Army, Navy and Air Force facilities, the major portion of Naval Academy candidates will be scheduled for examination at Naval Medical Examining Facilities. Candidates examined at Naval Medical Examining Facililies will normally be required to spend one day under examination. Candidates are to report prior to 0800 on the day of examination except as otherwise directed in reporting orders. Candidates ordered to Army and Air Force examining centers will be required to spend at least two days to complete examinations.

Candidates are required to pay their own transportation, berthing and necessary expenses in connection with these examinations. ONLY ONE MEDICAL AND PHYSICAL APTITUDE EXAMINATION WILL BE AUTHORIZED FOR ANY CANDIDATE. REEXAMINATION WILL NOT BE AUTHORIZED EXCEPT AS REQUIRED BY THE CHIEF OF NAVAL PERSONNEL.

303.3 Review and waiver procedure

The results of all medical examinations of candidates for the Naval Academy are subject to review by the Permanent Board of Medical Examiners, U.S. Naval Academy. Medical qualification decisions made by that Board are final. In this respect where the disqualifying defect is subject to medical or dental correction, the candidate may be conditionally rejected subject to later certification by a registered physician or dentist that the defect has been corrected with complete restoration of function. It is mandatory that such certification reach the Permanent Board of Medical Examiners as soon as possible and not later than 15 March in any case. Final reports of applicants certified by that Board will be distributed to Chief of Naval Personnel, Chief, Bureau of Medicine and Surgery, and the Academic Board, U.S. Naval Academy. The *Academic Board may grant waiver* of a very minor defect to a candidate who is outstanding in all other respects.

Since waiver action is predicated upon the overall quality of a candidate's record, it is important that transcripts of secondary school or college work, the report of extracurricular activities, and the required letters of recommendation be submitted as soon as possible. In some instances it will be necessary to delay evaluation of a record until results of the March College Board tests have been received. IT IS EMPHASIZED THAT REVIEW AND WAIVER PROCEDURES ARE AUTOMATIC FOR ALL CANDIDATES WHO WERE FOUND NOT MEDICALLY QUALIFIED UPON FORMAL QUALIFYING MEDICAL EXAMI-

NATION AND THAT QUERIES REGARDING THE STATUS OF WAIVER ACTION WILL ONLY DELAY FINAL DETERMINATION. Notification of Medical and Physical Aptitude Disqualification will be made to all candidates by the Chief of Naval Personnel. Requests for reexamination of those candidates who fail the medical examination can be approved only by the Chief of Naval Personnel and only under extremely extenuating circumstances.

Format for requesting a Congressional nomination

Date

Honorable		Honorable ....
House of Representatives	OR	United States Senate
Washington, D.C. 20025		Washington, D.C. 20025
Dear Mr.		Dear Senator ....

It is my desire to attend the United States Naval Academy and to make the United States Navy my career. I respectfully request that I be considered as one of your nominees for the class that enters the Academy in June 1965.

The following data are furnished for your information:

Name: (As recorded on birth certificate)

Address: (City, County, State)

Name of Parents:

Date of Birth:

High School Attended:

Date of High School Graduation:

Approximate Grade Average:

My high school transcript of work completed to date is attached. I have been active in high school extracurricular activities shown on the attached list.

I shall greatly appreciate your consideration of my request for a nomination to the U.S. Naval Academy.

Sincerely yours,

Signature

Format for requesting a Presidential nomination

Date

Chief of Naval Personnel
Department of the Navy
Washington, D.C. 20370

ATTN: Pers–B66

Dear Sir:

I request a nomination under the Presidential category for the class that enters the Naval Academy in June 1965 and submit the following information:

Name: (*Give name as shown on birth certificate. If different from that which you use, attach a copy of court order, if applicable.*)

Address: (*Give permanent and temporary address*)

Date of Birth: (*Spell out month*)

Date of High School Graduation:

If Member of Military: (*List rank, serial number, component, branch of service, and organizational address*)

If Previous Candidate: (*List year*)

Information on Parent

Name, Rank, Serial Number, Component and Branch of Service:

Organizational Address:

Retired or Deceased: (*Give date and attach copy of retirement orders or casualty report*)

Officer Personnel: (*Attach statement of service prepared by Personnel Officer specifying Regular or Reserve status for all periods of service*)

Enlisted Personnel: (*Attach statement prepared by Personnel Officer listing date of enlistment, date of expiration of enlistment, component and branch of service*)

Sincerely yours,

Signature

Format for requesting a son of deceased veteran nomination

Date

Chief of Naval Personnel
Department of the Navy
Washington, D.C. 20370

ATTN: Pers–B66

Dear Sir:

I request a nomination under the Sons of Deceased Veterans category for the class that enters the Naval Academy in June 1965 and submit the following information:

Name: (*Give name as shown on birth certificate. If different from that which you use, attach a copy of court order, if applicable.*)

Address: (*Give permanent and temporary address*)

Date of Birth: (*Spell out month*)

Date of High School Graduation:

If Member of Military: (*List rank, serial number, component, branch of service, and organizational address*)

If Previous Candidate: (*List year*)

Information on Parent

Name, Rank, Serial Number, Regular or Reserve Component and Branch of Service:

Date and Place of Death:

Cause of Death:

Veterans Administration XC Claim Number: (*Forwarding a copy of death certificate, preferably the casualty report, will expedite processing of your application*)

Address of VA Office where case is filed:

Sincerely yours,

Signature

Appendix B

Naval ROTC Units

Auburn University
Brown University
California, University of
California at Los Angeles, University of
Colorado, University of
Columbia University
Cornell University
Dartmouth College
Duke University
Georgia Institute of Technology
Harvard University
Holy Cross, College of the
Idaho, University of
Illinois Institute of Technology
Illinois, University of
Iowa State University of Science and Technology
Kansas, University of
Louisville, University of
Marquette University
Massachusetts Institute of Technology
Miami University
Michigan, University of
Minnesota, University of
Mississippi, University of
Missouri, University of
Nebraska, University of
New Mexico, University of
North Carolina, University of
Northwestern University
Notre Dame, University of
Ohio State University
Oklahoma, University of
Oregon State College
Pennsylvania State University
Pennsylvania, University of
Princeton University
Purdue University
Rensselaer Polytechnic Institute
Rice Institute
Rochester, University of
South Carolina, University of
Southern California, University of
Stanford University
Texas, University of
Tufts College
Tulane University of Louisiana
Utah, University of
Vanderbilt University
Villanova University
Virginia, University of
Washington, University of
Wisconsin, University of
Yale University

Bibliography

Of the books which I read while gathering material for this work, the following are those I believe of most interest and value to anyone who wants to learn more of the American naval profession and its origins.

BRODIE, Bernard. *A Guide to Naval Strategy*. Princeton: Princeton University Press, 1958.

FISKE, Bradley A. *From Midshipman to Rear Admiral.* New York: Century, 1919.

KING, Ernest J. and WHITEHILL, Walter Muir. *Fleet Admiral King: A Naval Record.* New York: Norton, 1952.

KNOX, Dudley W. *A History of the United States Navy*. New York: Putnam, 1948.

MAHAN, Alfred T. *From Sail to Steam.* New York: Harper, 1907.

MAHAN, Alfred T. *The Influence of Sea Power upon History, 1660–1783*. New York: Sagamore Press, 1957.

MORISON, Elting E. *Admiral Sims and the Modern American Navy*. Boston: Houghton Mifflin, 1942.

MORISON, Samuel E. *History of United States Naval Operations in World War II.* 15 vols. Boston: Little, Brown, 1947 to 1960.

MORISON, Samuel E. *John Paul Jones: A Sailor's Biography*. Boston: Little, Brown, 1959.

MORISON, Samuel E. *The Two-Ocean War*. Boston: Little, Brown, 1963.

PRATT, Fletcher. *The Navy: A History*. Garden City: Garden City, 1941.

PULESTON, William D. *Mahan: The Life and Work of Captain Alfred Thayer Mahan, USN*. New Haven: Yale University Press, 1939.

SPROUT, Harold and Margaret. *The Rise of American Naval Power, 1776–1918*. Princeton: Princeton University Press, 1944.

Index

About the Author

James Calvert is a native of Ohio, and grew up in the small town of Berlin Heights, near Cleveland. He attended Oberlin College and then entered the U.S. Naval Academy, from which he graduated in 1942. He served as executive officer of the submarine *Jack* during World War II, completed nine war patrols, and was awarded two Silver Star and two Bronze Star medals for his war service.

After the war he commanded the submarine *Trigger* and then was selected for training in nuclear submarines. Commanding the atomic-powered submarine *Skate* from her commissioning in 1957 until 1959, he took her on two pioneering voyages under the ice of the Arctic Ocean to the North Pole. In March of 1959 the *Skate* became the first ship in history to reach the surface of the Arctic Ocean at the North Pole. For his achievements with the *Skate*, he received three Legions of Merit and his ship was twice awarded the Navy Unit Commendation. His earlier book, *Surface at the Pole*, tells the story of these two voyages.

In June of 1965, after this book had gone to press, Calvert was selected for Rear Admiral, the second youngest officer to be so selected in the history of the Navy.

He is now on duty in the Pentagon.